PRODUCERS, PARASITES, PATRIOTS

PRODUCERS, PARASITES, PATRIOTS

● ● ●

RACE AND THE NEW RIGHT-WING POLITICS OF PRECARITY

● ● ●

DANIEL MARTINEZ HoSANG AND JOSEPH E. LOWNDES

University of Minnesota Press
Minneapolis ● *London*

Portions of the Introduction were previously published as "The Labor of Race in the Age of Inequality," in *Racism Postrace*, ed. Roopali Mukherjee, Sarah Banet-Weiser, and Herman Gray (Durham, N.C.: Duke University Press, 2018); reprinted by permission of the copyright holder, Duke University Press. Chapter 1 was previously published as "Parasites of Government: Racial Antistatism and Representations of Public Employees amid the Great Recession," *American Quarterly* 68, no. 4 (December 2016): 931–54; copyright 2016 The American Studies Association.

Published by the University of Minnesota Press
111 Third Avenue South, Suite 290
Minneapolis, MN 55401-2520
http://www.upress.umn.edu

Printed in the United States of America on acid-free paper

The University of Minnesota is an equal-opportunity educator and employer.

26 25 24 23 22 21 20 19   10 9 8 7 6 5 4 3 2 1

Library of Congress Cataloging-in-Publication Data

Names: HoSang, Daniel, author. | Lowndes, Joseph E., author.
Title: Producers, parasites, patriots : race and the new right-wing politics of
    precarity / Daniel Martinez HoSang, Joseph E. Lowndes.
Description: Minneapolis : University of Minnesota Press, 2019. | Includes
    bibliographical references and index. |
Identifiers: LCCN 2018045508 (print) | ISBN 978-1-5179-0358-9 (hc) |
    ISBN 978-1-5179-0359-6 (pb)
Subjects: LCSH: United States—Race relations—History—21st century. |
    Social structure—United States—History—21st century. | Global Financial
    Crisis, 2008–2009. | Right and left (Political science). | BISAC: POLITICAL
    SCIENCE / Political Ideologies / Conservatism & Liberalism. | SOCIAL
    SCIENCE / Discrimination & Race Relations. | SOCIAL SCIENCE / Social
    Classes.
Classification: LCC E184.A1 .H658 2019 (print) | DDC 305.800973—dc23
LC record available at https://lccn.loc.gov/2018045508

CONTENTS

INTRODUCTION

The Changing Labor of Race
in the New Gilded Age

• • •

We met Joey Gibson in 2018 on a warm April afternoon on the fourth-floor terrace of a public library overlooking Vancouver, Washington—a bedroom community just over the Columbia River from Portland, Oregon. We came to interview Gibson, an activist who had recently launched a campaign for a U.S. Senate seat, about what had inspired his "anti-establishment" crusade. Gibson told us that Jesus, as "a revolutionary rebel," was his first inspiration, "and then, obviously, Martin Luther King, with him preaching love and peace and nonviolent resistance. A lot of stuff that he did is stuff that I have been trying to do." He went on to describe the impact of watching the Black student sit-ins in Greensboro, North Carolina, in 1960: "I've seen the videos of them going into the diner millions of times and taking that beating, and it's amazing because you see them get knocked to the ground, you think they're done, and they just sit down again and they just take it." As we conversed about contemporary political problems, Gibson referred to mass incarceration as "legal slavery," saying that "mandatory minimum sentencing is horrible. It's devastating. It's been completely disruptive to the Black community. Do we really need to put all these people in a jail cell and take away their freedoms because they have an addiction? It's crazy to me."[1]

There would be nothing surprising in hearing a progressive political activist cite Martin Luther King Jr. or the lunch counter sit-ins as inspirations, or connecting mass incarceration to slavery.

The civil rights movement continues to stand as the most iconic social movement in the United States, and mass imprisonment has been in the foreground of social justice activism in the past decade. But Joey Gibson is neither a progressive nor a social justice activist. On the contrary, he dwells politically on the furthest shores of the American right. The organization he founded, Patriot Prayer, became synonymous with violent demonstrations after Trump's election in 2016 and made Gibson one of the most notorious far-right figures in the nation. Gibson organized regular "free speech" and "pro-Trump" rallies throughout 2017 that drew members of white-supremacist groups, including the Ku Klux Klan and Identity Evropa, and featured racist speakers and renowned streetfighters. These rallies, where attendees regularly adorned themselves in body armor and homemade weapons and where extra security was often provided by groups such as the protofascist Proud Boys and the heavily armed Three Percenters militia, often resulted in bloody assaults on antiracists and antifascists who showed up to oppose them.[2] Patriot Prayer attracted, among others, Jeremy Christian, the white supremacist who stabbed two people to death and severely injured a third who sought to stop him from harassing two Muslim women on a Portland light rail train in May 2017. Christian had attended one of Gibson's rallies two weeks prior to the murder, wearing an American Revolutionary War flag as a cape and giving Nazi salutes to counter-protestors. As the city reeled from Christian's grisly killings, Gibson went ahead with plans for another rally just days after.[3] In the summer of 2018, Gibson continued to organize a series of mass rallies in Portland and Seattle seeking to galvanize a vigilante movement of the far right, a street Trumpism bound together by a violent antipathy toward the left.[4]

How do we square the Joey Gibson whose campaign web page features an image of civil rights marchers in Selma kneeling in prayer with the Joey Gibson who helped spawn a political milieu populated by violent Islamophobes, white nationalists, and fascist street brawlers? What kind of political labor is performed by an invocation of the Black freedom struggle by a figure on the far right? And how do we account for the continued presence of a small but consistent number of men of color, including Gibson, in

Home page of the Joey Gibson Senate Campaign website, www.gibsonforfreedom.com. May 31, 2018.

the central leadership of these groups, some of whom even pose for photos making "white power" gestures?[5]

Stories like Gibson's and the questions they raise are what prompted us to write this book. They speak to the aporias of this moment in U.S. politics and to the new deployments of racial meaning by the right in a moment of growing economic precarity. Across the landscape we see many surprising scenarios: white public-sector workers depicted as "the new welfare queens";[6] impoverished whites in the "opioid belt" described as culturally and genetically inferior populations; Black and brown Tea Partiers hailed as the new leaders of an overwhelmingly white conservative movement; and far-right figures like Gibson imagining themselves to be inheritors of the civil rights movement, paradoxically conjoining non-whiteness with invocations of white supremacy.

Do these disorienting examples lend credence to the idea that we have now entered a postracial society? Quite the opposite. In a polity founded on African slavery, imperial expansion, and Native dispossession, the idea of "race" has shaped every aspect of political development in U.S. history structurally, institutionally, and culturally.

Indeed, the stories we tell in *Producers, Parasites, Patriots* underscore the fundamental role that race continues to play in reproducing and naturalizing the growing social, political, and economic inequalities marking the current moment. Though our title foregrounds the *right-wing* politics of precarity, this book is not limited to self-described actors on the right (though they are a significant part of the story). We also use *right-wing* to denote the broad ways that vulnerability, suffering, and premature death become socially legible. The racialized categories of the "producer," the "parasite," and the "patriot" have long been deployed to do this work, differentiating those groups deemed self-reliant, autonomous, and worthy of social protection from those who are dependent, debased, and worthy of abandonment and disavowal. As we argue below, changing material and political conditions have produced subtle but significant shifts in the ways these categories are put to use and inhabited.

Race and Class in the New Gilded Age

These dynamics remind us, however, that we are in the midst of a new and distinct conjuncture in the United States composed of at least two major phenomena. The first is the rise of what some scholars have deemed a "New Gilded Age," which marks the great acceleration of material inequality and the movement of the U.S. state toward autocracy.[7] Political and economic power is concentrated at the very top in historically novel ways after a half century of decline in public provision and wealth redistribution. Decades of stagnant or declining wages, privatization, and deregulation coupled with profound levels of personal debt have had devastating effects on low- and middle-income households; the post-2009 recovery still left forty million households living below the poverty line at the end of the Obama presidency. In 2016, the Federal Reserve reported that the top 10 percent of the population owned 77 percent of the wealth, with the rest distributed among the bottom 90 percent.[8] In this context, elite influence over electoral politics, public policy, education, media, and cultural institutions has intensified.

The second element we examine is the transformation of the meanings and *labor* of *race* in the post–civil rights era. Malcolm X famously noted that "racism is like a Cadillac, they bring out a new model every year."[9] While racial subordination is an enduring feature of U.S. political history, it continually changes in response to shifting social and political conditions, interests, and structures. In this moment, racial disparities along many indices are at historically high levels even as racial inequality is everywhere denounced. At the same time, elite powers and interests from across the political spectrum have become invested in a symbolic form of multiculturalism and racial pluralism that was unimaginable a half century ago. The Heritage Foundation, long the ideological compass of the conservative movement, is today presided over by a Black woman. A book recently published by the libertarian Cato Institute celebrates the abolitionist Frederick Douglass as a "self-made man," an idealized neoliberal subject who was never in support of "the interests of the collective."[10] These new modes of incorporation have done nothing to redistribute resources and power more equitably, but they have permitted elites to deploy narratives of racial uplift and difference in ways that legitimate their own authority.

As the cultural theorists Stuart Hall and Doreen Massey note, the shaping of popular consciousness and consent often compels those in power "to detach concepts from their previous associations and shift them to new meanings."[11] The civil rights era made some expressions of white supremacy contestable in public life. It also offered new framings of antiracism and racial uplift as exemplars of national exceptionalism and virtue that could be claimed by a broad array of movements, actors, and ideologies. And as the United States becomes more racially diverse, political elites in general and conservatives in particular require new ways of incorporating non-white symbols, narratives, and people. Political and economic elites need novel forms of moral legitimation to justify the withdrawal of their commitments to the growing number of households newly vulnerable to an economy rooted in plunder and financial predation. This legitimation has increasingly come in the form of incorporating the discourse and settled meanings from the civil rights movement wherein redemptive deployments of racial difference in general and Blackness in particular become crucial strategies of governance.

The consequences of the post–civil rights era and the post–New Deal era are entwined in this period in ways that both reinforce old racial hierarchies and open the door for new kinds of racial signification. Race performs dynamic and often contradictory work, continuing to produce hierarchy and exclusion while also generating new forms of mobility and incorporation. Like all forms of popular common sense, racism is a composite formation, bearing vestiges of bygone dynamics as well as traces of emerging developments.[12] The contradictions in this moment confront us everywhere.

In the United States today there is an intensification of racialized aggression against people of color not seen since the massive resistance to the civil rights movement in the mid-twentieth century. These open racial threats have come up from the streets and down from the state. Black and brown communities face continual state predation, abandonment, and violence—and now, newly energized white-supremacist attacks. Overt and unapologetic expressions of white supremacy are on the rise, as are crimes of racial violence and terror, particularly against women and LGBT people of color.[13] In August 2017 the United Nations issued an "early warning" on the state of racial discrimination in the United States, an admonition that in the last decade has only been issued to conflict in states such as Burundi, Iraq, Ivory Coast, Kyrgyzstan, and Nigeria.[14]

This intensified racialized domination occurs at a moment when the United States is undergoing the most massive upward transfer of wealth it has experienced since the Gilded Age of the late nineteenth century. The institutions that for much of the twentieth century served to guard against the upward redistribution of wealth—labor unions, progressive income and wealth taxation policies, social welfare programs, consumer protections, and civil rights and anti-discrimination laws—have faced sustained attacks and have become dramatically weakened.

The starkness of these conditions should provide an extraordinary opportunity for those committed to a vision of economic redistribution and antiracism. And yet in our politics and in our thinking, it seems we inevitably collapse back into a class/race divide when attempting to understand and engage the politics of precarity with which we are faced. While there is important nuance and distinction in the extant scholarship, two important theoretical formations are worth exploring in brief. The prevailing framework used to interpret inequalities in resources and power for many political historians and social scientists who study race has been predicated on an understanding of dueling racial orders, traditions, or visions of nationhood competing for authority. In this view, there is an objective racial antagonism—often metonymically represented as W. E. B. Du Bois's "problem of the color line"— that has fundamentally shaped politics and society since the era of modern slavery and colonization.[15]

These accounts vary in their particular renderings and detail, but this framework often maps a conflict between an egalitarian, liberal, and inclusive antiracist political bloc on the one hand and a hierarchical and conservative racist bloc on the other. Contemporary accounts of racial disparities—in wealth, income, incarceration rates, health outcomes, and education—further index this opposition. The "New Jim Crow" of the prison system or the racialized "achievement gap" in education, for example, can ultimately be traced back to the antagonism of the color line. This analysis is rooted in claims about the micropolitics of racial antagonism (including recent attention to unconscious bias and micro-aggression) as well as systemic analyses of institutional and structural racism. Such analyses include much of the mainstream scholarship in ethnic studies, the race subfields of the social sciences, and many activist formations.[16]

By contrast, an alternative analysis interprets political and economic inequality as an effect of divergent and antagonistic class interests. From this perspective, the overrepresentation of African Americans and Latino/as among the nation's working poor and economically destitute is primarily a manifestation not of the antagonism of the color line but rather of the imperatives of capital in an era of financialization, continued deindustrialization, and widening inequality. While this analysis has long held currency in materialist studies of slavery and U.S. industrialization, it has received renewed attention in several works by an influential group of scholars grounded in African American history and politics who point to the ways race now operates primarily to

mask or mystify class antagonisms. Barbara Fields and Karen
Fields have referred to this process as "racecraft"—a "mental terrain" and "persuasive belief" that functions as a folk ideology and
more closely parallels the epistemology of seventeenth-century
witchcraft than any contemporary social-scientific inquiry.[17] The
political scientist Adolph Reed similarly argues that contemporary
antiracist formations, largely emptied of their oppositional politics, are as likely to abet the upward redistribution of wealth as to
resist it.[18] The historian Jacqueline Jones positions race itself as a
national "creation myth" that legitimates contemporary forms of
economic inequality: "Today, certain groups of people are impoverished, exploited in the workplace, or incarcerated in large numbers. This is not the case because of their 'race,' however, but
rather because at a particular point in US history certain other
groups began to invoke the myth of race in a bid for economic
and political power."[19] From this perspective, it is economic inequality and the exploitation of labor demanded under market
economies that produces the race concept as ideologically salient
and socially useful. In short, racial inequality can be defined as a
by-product of capitalist accumulation.

Coproductions of Race and Class

In a generative 1980 essay titled "Race, Articulation, and Societies Structured in Dominance," Stuart Hall calls for "an analysis
of the specific forms which racism assumes in its ideological functioning" in relation to "the dominant class relations." He argues
for an attention to the specific ways in which racism "secures a
whole social formation under a dominant class" within particular
historic conditions.[20] Like Reed, Fields and Fields, and Jones, Hall
insists that an analysis of race can never be abstracted from the
antagonisms produced by class conflict and exploitation. But for
Hall, race plays a critical and historically specific ideological role
in this process, often becoming the "modality in which class is
'lived,' the form in which it is appropriated and 'fought through.'"[21]
Hall notes the particular ideological labor that race often performs within a society "structured in dominance." He explains

that "racism discovers what other ideologies have to construct: an apparently 'natural' and universal basis in nature itself. . . . [I]t articulates securely with an us/them structure of corporate class consciousness. . . . [R]acisms also dehistoricize—translating historically-specific structures into the timeless language of nature."[22] It is not merely that racialized domination is historically produced and continually reinforced by capitalism. Capitalism has historically depended on racialization to produce class rule and stymie the promise of democracy. Race plays a critical role in constituting the political subjects of a capitalist economy, making legible the range of political roles—tied to capacities for autonomy, self-regulation, and ownership on the one hand and dependence, indolence, and subservience on the other—necessary to reproduce capitalism itself. As Ruth Wilson Gilmore explains, "capitalism requires inequality and racism enshrines it."[23]

Hall's insights lay much of the groundwork for contemporary scholars attempting to theorize the particular political work of race in the context of widening economic inequalities and militarized and carceral state control. The practices of neoliberalism— valorizing the market, reorganizing the state, ending downward redistribution, removing protections—have entailed specific constructs of autonomy, dependency, and worth. As Lisa Duggan asserts, "neoliberalism has assembled its projects and interests from the field of issues saturated with race, with gender, with sex, with religion, with ethnicity, and nationality."[24] Jodi Melamed has argued that neoliberal policy itself "engenders new racial subjects, as it creates and distinguishes between newly privileged and stigmatized collectivities, yet multiculturalism codes the wealth, mobility, and political power of neoliberalism's beneficiaries to be the just desserts of 'multicultural world citizens,' while representing those that neoliberalism dispossesses to be handicapped by their own 'monoculturalism' or other historico-cultural deficiencies."[25] Neoliberal multiculturalism performs historically specific work by "breaking with an older racism's reliance on phenotype to innovate new ways of fixing human capacities to naturalize inequality. The new racism deploys economic, ideological, cultural, and religious distinctions to produce lesser personhoods, laying these new categories of privilege and stigma across conventional racial categories, fracturing them into differential status groups."[26]

An important body of scholarship and political activism in the twentieth century popularized the contention that racial groupings, boundaries, and meanings are socially constructed rather than expressive of group-based biological or genetic difference. Race is a social construction, to be sure. But we argue that it is more particularly a *political* construction, generated by historically specific structures of power. Any society "structured in dominance" requires a shared basis of comprehending and reproducing distinctions of merit and stigma, autonomy and dependency, and authority and dispossession. Within the United States, conceptualizations of race have always provided a legitimating vocabulary and grammar. The value afforded to various categories of labor (honorable or degraded), the status of capital (heroic or parasitic), and the relationship forged between state and market all depend upon such distinctions. Claims about dependency, autonomy, and freedom have always been constructed through racialized and gendered meaning and references. Thus, as we demonstrate, even when these claims are used to stigmatize groups of largely white workers, race still performs important political labor, as the hierarchical taxonomies of capitalism continue to be constituted through racialized distinctions and meanings. *Producers, Parasites, Patriots* builds on the scholarship and analysis of Hall, Melamed, Gilmore, and others as an analysis of the mutually generative relationship between race and class, one that highlights the surprising ways that each is mobilized by the right under current circumstances.

The Constraints of Civil Rights

This moment demands new analytic frames for understanding the relationship between race, class, and state institutions. Since the end of World War II, both the main scholarly works on race within the United States and the major political projects committed to civil rights and racial justice have been premised on a set of assumptions about the capacities of the U.S. state and economy and the possibilities of inclusion within both: an expanding economy that can produce enough surplus to ensure the continued stability of key institutional formations (including education, criminal justice, health care, environmental management, the military, and representative government) in a way that could incorporate new racialized subjects.

In this context, antiracist political strategies, scholarship, and analyses have generally been centered on eradicating racial bias and exclusion through the enforcement of anti-discrimination laws in order to win access to institutions and resources for racially subordinated groups. In a period when the overall U.S. economy continued to grow, promising higher wages and standards of living to each new generation, and as U.S. institutions were regarded as guarantors of a well-functioning civil society, those assumptions seemed fully warranted. Thus, struggles over affirmative action, housing desegregation, employment discrimination, voting rights, and access to resources and services were all premised on both the effectiveness of the relevant institutions and access to a surplus, especially in the form of public budgets, capable of financing these efforts.

It is increasingly evident, however, that these conditions can no longer be presumed. For example, when the University of California's affirmative action programs were first challenged in the late 1970s by a white medical-school applicant named Allan Bakke, the institution itself was well financed and prosperous—providing an affordable and accessible education to students and secure employment to tens of thousands of people. While the struggle over affirmative action continues today in that state, the institution itself has experienced dramatic change, characterized by steep increases in tuition and student debt, the rise of the contingent academic workforce, and continual disinvestment by the state.[27]

The accelerating wealth and income gap, along with four decades of privatization, deregulation, and regressive tax policy, has essentially removed a large proportion of economic surplus from the authority of the state and thus from the demands of racially subordinated groups. The institutions and sectors that have historically been the subject of racial-justice activism—schools, representative government, public- and private-sector employment—are themselves in deep crisis. And in an age of permanent war, global migration and displacement, and ecological crisis, the question posed by James Baldwin more than fifty years ago, "Do I really want to be integrated into a burning house?" takes on new urgency and meaning.[28] A racial-justice analysis focused on institutional inclusion and incorporation can no longer ignore these conditions. At the same time, many white people who have long been invested in the protections afforded to them by the "color line" are facing new conditions of precarity, deprivations that have long been familiar to subordinated groups in the United States.

Racial Transposition

Autonomy versus dependency, producer versus parasite, virtue versus vice, individual versus collective, and fitness versus weakness are among the main binaries that have generated racial categories in the United States and shored up its hierarchies in a capitalist society. In our analysis we foreground the use of these binaries as they have been mutually constituted through the formation of Blackness and whiteness in the post–New Deal era, along with the concomitant (and contradictory) emergence of the broadly accepted moral authority of the mainstream civil rights movement.

We use the term *racial transposition* across this book to name the varied ways in which representations of racial meaning travel and circulate. It describes a process through which the meaning, valence, and signification of race can be transferred from one context, group, or setting to another, shaping the ways in which racial categories structure broad fields of social meaning. The concept extends historian Natalia Molina's notion of "racial scripts"—the complex of racialized significations ascribed to one group which, Molina explains, "can easily be transferred to new groups." Molina cautions that "these scripts are not automatically uprooted from one situation to the next or simply transferred from one group to another. We must always take into consideration the conditions under which racial scripts emerge—the social structure, the material conditions, and the historical context—and bear in mind that there is not a uniform experience of racialization, which varies by national origins, immigrant status, skin color, language acquisition, and perception of foreignness, for example."[29] Race, in other words, is not open to any sort of signification for any given body or group. Race is determined, ultimately, by the history from which it emerges and the play of political forces to which it is subject.[30]

Transpositions of race are not a new phenomenon, and the grammar and structure of the process have been well documented by other scholars. The broad history of colonialism, slavery, and settlement has been structured through efforts to differentiate people from one another into distinct and socially legible racial categories, but those distinctions are always shifting. In *Black Marxism*, Cedric Robinson demonstrates that the "emergence of racial order in feudal Europe" shaped (or in our terms, was transposed upon) the system of racial capitalism that expanded beyond Europe. As Robinson explains: "The tendency of European civilization through capitalism was thus not to homogenize but to differentiate—to exaggerate regional, subcultural, and dialectical differences into 'racial' ones. As the Slavs became the natural slaves, the racially inferior stock for domination and exploitation during the early Middle Ages, as the Tartars came to occupy a similar position in the Italian cities of the late Middle Ages, so at the systemic interlocking of capitalism in the sixteenth century, the peoples of the Third World began to fill this expanding category of a civilization reproduced by capitalism."[31] What's important to note here is Robinson's emphasis that the "category" of inferiority that is necessitated by capitalism has existed prior to Europe's encounter with "the peoples of the Third World." By attending to the continuities in the classificatory and taxonomic categories of capitalism, we can understand how the social and political meanings signified by "race" can travel across place and time.

Similarly, Molina explains that many of the formative debates within immigration law and public policy in the early twentieth century involved processes in which the characteristics associated with one racialized group were brought to bear on another as a way of establishing their social standing and value. For example, the social meaning and standing of "Mexican" as a racial category was established over time through constructions of Blackness, whiteness, and indigeneity.[32]

More recently, Donald Trump's statement at a White House event on immigration in May 2018 that some people entering the United States were "not people" but "animals"[33] circulated within a field of racist discourse that has sought to represent Blackness as outside the sphere of humanity. Indeed, the intensification of immigrant detention, deportation, and incarceration that has targeted migrants from the Global South more generally has drawn from narratives of degeneracy and incorrigibility that had long justified Black subordination.[34] While our analysis of racial transposition often centers on Blackness, the field of contemporary racial politics and racial formation has also shaped and been shaped by other racialized phenomena. These include the rise of non-European immigration to the United States since 1965 and the parallel growth in nativist political projects, as well as the post-9/11 intensification of Islamophobia.

As we emphasize throughout the book, racial transposition does not render or situate groups within equivalent social positions. The transposition of particular characteristics from one group to another does not transform group-based structures of racial power and domination. To argue that some white workers have become newly stigmatized through the deployment of narratives and representations once reserved for people of color in general and Black people in particular is not to argue that their social and political standing is equivalent or somehow converging. Whiteness still affords a host of political protections and indemnifications, but they are not absolute.

Our examination of the shifting terrain of white precarity necessarily entails an interrogation of the specific histories of anti-Black racial projects. As the political scientist Tiffany Willoughby-Herard explains, "the construction of the abject black other and the construction of white poverty are inextricably bound together but not the same."[35] Whiteness no longer ensures indemnification from charges of civic failure and social abandonment, but those narratives are only legible because they have been long deployed to construct "the abject black other."

There are two interrelated articulations of Blackness within the field of politics, governance, and state formation examined in this book, what we might call the signifying political labor of Blackness. In the dominant mode, Blackness functions as the negation of the polity—that which is outside the realm of state protection and recognized civic life. Black abjection in this modality provides the boundary condition through which civic life is constituted, and it continues to be foundational to the reproduction of state authority and power. We can witness its effects across multiple spheres—mass incarceration, labor exploitation, policing, the denial of reproductive autonomy, education, social welfare, housing segregation, and employment. While its language and terms have evolved, this expulsion of Blackness from the polity is indispensable not only to the regulation and control of Black communities but also to the deference and consent of non-Black communities.

But we also explore a related process, one that is productive of a redemptive subjectivity, in which Blackness becomes represented as the ethical embodiment of a distinctly American national identity and exceptionalism. Here, the histories of Black abjection and subordination paradoxically authorize the selective valorization of some Black figures. These figures are summoned and valorized to testify to the enduring qualities and virtues of the nation, the exemplars of individualistic striving and persistence in the face of hostility and institutional failure. Thus, long-standing narratives of Black uplift and the moral perseverance of the civil rights movement are repurposed to defend and naturalize markets and militarized national authority, redefining neoliberalism as a form of antiracist freedom, even as the large majority of Black people face worsening dispossession, violence, and abandonment.

Barack Obama's political rise exemplified these dual modalities, as he was represented as both a fantasized racial threat to American national identity (either as a socialist or foreign-born usurper) and as the clearest evidence of national redemption and exceptionalism. The steady uptick in the number of high-profile Black figures within contemporary conservative political formations described in chapter 3 has been a key site in reproducing and legitimating neoliberal conservative policies along the lines of the latter.

In the chapters that follow, we consider the contradictory uses of race by political actors and organizations on the right in relation to contemporary political and economic conditions. Through careful analyses of diverse political sites and conflicts—attacks on public-sector unions, the ascent of elites of color, and new framings to explain white precarity—we highlight new deployments of race on the right in the ascendant age of inequality. Ultimately, we argue against the tendency in dominant scholarly debates to pit race against class in evaluating the central determinants of inequality. The reorganization of the global economy and the upward redistribution of wealth, resources, and power are modulated through racial meaning and categories. Race continues to structure the terms of political identity, mobilization, and responses to economic vulnerability, though in ways quite distinct from the dominant patterns of the post–World War II era.

Our first chapter examines cultural representations of race deployed in attacks against public employees during the Great Recession. Beginning in 2009, a chorus of critics on the right charged that unionized public employees were becoming "parasites of government" who consumed tax dollars and productive labor to subsidize a profligate lifestyle. By analyzing a series of discursive representations—political cartoons, television comedy skits, political advertisements and speeches—we demonstrate the ways in which constructions of parasitism have become transposed onto white public-sector workers, including teachers, lifeguards, and firefighters, who have traditionally been exempt from such charges. These attacks reflect the most recent development of an antistatist politics that had historically assailed the redistributive state through its association with racialized dependents.

In chapter 2 we explore the contradictory ways in which white political identity becomes inhabited and politically invoked in the context of long-term abandonment. Middle- and working-class whites, like other demographic groups in the United States, have been subject to static or declining wages over the last forty years, are working longer hours for less and less, and have seen state support in the form social services evaporate. Conservatives, who came to power from the late 1960s onward through the support of significant sectors of the white working class, have now largely abandoned them. One response has been exuberant support for Donald Trump's 2016 presidential bid. Meanwhile, conservative scholars and pundits have begun to describe the white poor in language once reserved for people of color—depicting them as socially disorganized, culturally deficient, and even genetically compromised.

The rise of a new cohort of Black politicians in visible positions within the Republican Party and other conservative formations is the focus of chapter 3, where we contend that this phenomenon is neither simply a tactical measure nor symbolic window dressing. Instead, we see in it more profound changes within both the dominant modes of neoliberal governance and important shifts in oppositional social movements. At stake here is the long-standing articulation of Blackness as an ethical subjectivity and mode of political critique, one that can either destabilize or naturalize particular configurations of power. On the one hand, the contemporary GOP is among the most right-wing and racially homogeneous major electoral parties in the nation's history. Racist appeals and alignments continue to structure the GOP's policy agenda and modes of address, as continued debates over immigration, police violence, Islamophobia, voter registration, and affirmative action demonstrate. On the other hand, as claims to whiteness no longer protect many white people against charges of parasitism or dependence, and provide fewer material guarantees in general, it is instructive that within the field of electoral politics and governance a growing number of people of color have become valorized as the standard-bearers for a producerist and patriotic anti-statism.

In chapter 4 we take up what may be the hardest case for racial transposition, the rise of far-right nationalism in the United States. Yet even here we see race at work in surprising ways. The far right in the United States, which always depends on a potent politics of white supremacy, is also increasingly shored up by symbols, narratives, and visible participation of people of color. From the 2016 Trump campaign to alt-right and alt-lite formations to open white nationalists, multiculturalism is deployed to shore up far-right political projects.

In chapter 5 we discuss the early 2016 occupation of the Malheur National Wildlife Refuge in eastern Oregon by armed militia groups seeking a confrontation with federal authorities over land use. We explore the connections—and disconnections—between conditions in the area surrounding Malheur and those marking predominantly Black communities like Flint, Michigan, and Ferguson, Missouri, that have also recently witnessed popular insurgencies. Like these areas, many parts of rural Oregon have been decimated by unemployment and economic crisis. But the legacies of white producerism, we argue, prevent the kind of transformative and far-reaching analyses and demands witnessed in Flint, Ferguson, and more generally within the Movement for Black Lives. What, then, might white rural Oregonians learn from traditions of Black organizing and political analysis to address their own conditions of precarity?

In the Conclusion we reflect on some normative implications of our study and consider the possibility of other forms of identification in which white subjects choose to align with progressive political projects led by and from communities of color because it is in these locations that the political analysis, organization, and legacies of opposition are most capable of producing resistance to privatization and abandonment. From this perspective, white efforts to promote racial justice are not realized through bland forms of "allyship" to support people of color around "their issues" but forged through a recognition of the interdependence between racially subordinated communities fighting their abandonment and heightened forms of white precarity. Resisting state violence, reversing privatization, reclaiming the public realm, and advancing democratic control of public institutions will require the articulation of a political vision that seeks the simultaneous end of both white supremacy and class rule. As we suggest, failure to do so may well enable new forms of both.

1
"PARASITES OF GOVERNMENT"
Racialized Anti-statism and
White Producerism

• • •

In early 2011, amid the mounting job losses and growing budget deficits of the Great Recession, the conservative radio commentator Rush Limbaugh took to the air to warn his listeners of a group of "freeloaders" who "live off of your tax payments and they want more. . . . They don't produce anything. They live solely off the output of the private sector."[1] They were, he explained on another show, "parasites of government."[2] Wisconsin governor Scott Walker described members of the same group as the "haves" and "taxpayers who foot the bills" as the "have-nots."[3] Indiana's governor, Mitch Daniels, labeled the group's members "a new privileged class in America."[4]

The charges rehearsed by Limbaugh and others draw from an enduring discourse of producerism within U.S. political culture, in which the virtuous, striving, and browbeaten producer struggles to fend off the parasite, a dependent subject that consumes tax dollars and productive labor to subsidize a profligate and extravagant lifestyle.[5] These representations have long been racialized and gendered; subjects marked as "welfare queens" and "illegal aliens" among others have been similarly condemned as freeloaders and parasites who feed off the labor of hardworking (white) taxpayers.[6]

The focus of Limbaugh's scorn, however, was a group of wage earners rarely represented on the latter side of the producerist/parasite divide: public-sector workers and their unions. While women and people of color constitute a larger proportion of state and municipal workers in comparison to the private sector, in 2011, 70 percent of this workforce was still identified as white and nearly a third were white men.[7] Indeed, in Wisconsin, the site of the highest-profile attack on public-sector workers during the Great Recession, whites were slightly overrepresented in the public-sector workforce compared to the overall population of the state, while Black and Latino workers were slightly underrepresented.[8] Yet their whiteness did not indemnify significant numbers of public-sector workers from these attacks. Emergency workers, city and county employees, teachers, and other school employees became increasingly criticized as parasitic—threats to the body politic. As Minnesota governor Tim Pawlenty explained after the election, "Unionized public employees are making more money, receiving more generous benefits, and enjoying greater job security than the working families forced to pay for it with ever-higher taxes, deficits and debt."[9] These charges came from across the political spectrum, as Democratic governors including California's Jerry Brown and New York's Andrew Cuomo and Republicans such as New Jersey's Chris Christie and Ohio's John Kasich all maintained that taxpayers could no longer meet the allegedly insatiable demands of public-sector workers. Proposals to renegotiate or eliminate union contracts and to retract collective bargaining rights suddenly moved to the center of political debate in many states.[10]

How did public-sector workers come so easily to symbolize the cause of the 2008 recession and thus become the object of widespread political attack? They reflect, we argue, the most recent development of a racialized anti-statist politics yoked to a long-term effort to restrain the social wage and to privatize public goods.[11] The rise of the modern right in the United States was articulated through an antipathy to state power in which the redistributive state as a whole was stigmatized through its association with racialized dependents.[12] With the demobilization of the Black freedom movement in particular and the withering of the welfare state in general, anti-statist projects have sought to extend this logic to white beneficiaries of state action. Thus, in the contemporary age of inequality, commitments to public benefits and subsidies to white households, workers, and families that were long guaranteed in the postwar era have become newly vulnerable.[13]

We demonstrate this argument through an analysis of cultural representations of public-sector workers during the Great Recession, including syndicated political cartoons, television shows, political advertisements, and political speeches. These sources reveal the quotidian production of political identity and interest—the micropolitical processes that generate political meaning in everyday life—and explicate the cultural logics that make such identities and interests legible.

Race and the Ascendant Criticism of Public-Sector Workers

Political criticism of public-sector workers and labor unions has a long history, particularly among conservative groups and activists. As Steve Fraser and Joshua Freeman have contended, this opposition has been premised on a range of arguments, from the alleged threat they posed to principles of sovereign governance (which formed the basis of Franklin Roosevelt's opposition to such unions) to their complicity in extending the reach and scale of the welfare state.[14] Nelson Lichtenstein and Elizabeth Shermer maintain that "hostility to labor unions per se was a crystallizing impulse for the modern American Conservative movement . . . reaching back past the 1970s to the aftermath of the 1886 Haymarket Riot and through the 1920s American Plan, the backlash against Operation Dixie in the 1940s, and the political ascendancy of both Barry Goldwater and Ronald Reagan."[15] Throughout the 1980s and 1990s, conservative policy organizations elaborated the case for policy reforms necessary to undermine the influence of public-sector unions and to shrink public-sector employment more generally, arguing that the "rent-seeking" behavior of such unions came at the expense of taxpayers' interests.[16]

Lichtenstein and Shermer explain that historically it has been the ideological and policy agenda of public-sector unions that conservative forces have rallied against: "social solidarity, employment stability, limits on the workplace power of corporate management, plus a defense of the welfare state, progressive taxation, financial regulation, and a government apparatus energetic enough to supervise the health and safety of millions of American workers and consumers."[17] In these arguments, public-sector unionism threatened a set of abstract principles—freedom of association and choice, government sovereignty, economic competitiveness, and a fear of corruption—viewed as fundamental to a free-market economy. Other opponents assailed public-sector unions as narrow interest groups seeking to unduly influence government policy for their own gain.

The recent uptick in anti-union sentiment, however, differs in several important ways from previous rounds of anti-union political attacks. Whereas earlier criticisms focused primarily on the structural relationships and interests that public-sector unions allegedly sought to exploit, the current attacks make moral and characterological claims about public-sector workers themselves. This emphasis on the ethical deficiencies of public-sector workers, central to all of the examples discussed below, represents a new terrain of political attack and critique. In these accounts, public-sector workers are not only opportunistic political interests but also cultural miscreants—a gluttonous class of people living beyond the rules that apply to others. To take one representative example from California, Steven Greenhut, a widely read columnist in the *Orange County Register*, alleged in a 2008 piece titled "Out of the Way, Peasants" that special license plates afforded to some government workers effectively exempted them from all driving laws: "California has about 1 million citizens who are literally above the law. Members of this group . . . can drive their cars as fast as they choose. They can drink a six-pack of beer at a bar and then get behind the wheel and weave their way home. . . . Chances are they will never have to pay a fine or get a traffic citation."[18] In his 2009 book *Plunder! How Public Employee Unions Are Raiding Treasuries, Controlling Our Lives and Bankrupting the Nation*, Greenhut states this claim plainly: "Yes rank has its privileges, and it's clear that government workers have a rank above the rest of us."[19]

The association of public-sector workers with the state is central to these confrontations as well. In Wisconsin in 2011, Governor Walker insisted that he had no objections to private-sector unions and said that he would not support proposals that took aim at such workers. It was unionized government workers, he argued, whose wage and benefit gains came at the expense of the taxpayers he was elected to protect.[20] Rush Limbaugh similarly insisted public-employee unions are "are not private sector union people. These are people that live off of your tax payments. And they want more. They want you to have to pay more taxes so that they continue in their freeloader gigs."[21] Thus, the new round of attacks on public-sector unions gained particular purchase by drawing on a broader politics of taxpayers' rights and critiques of state excess.

These allegations draw on resonant themes in U.S. political culture of anti-statism, market-based individualism, and right-wing populism. As Chip Berlet and Matthew N. Lyons and others have argued, the category of "lazy parasites" threatening the producerist ethic has almost always been imagined as a racialized class including mothers on welfare, immigrants, and the undeserving poor.[22] White workers, especially those in public-sector jobs such as firefighters, teachers, and transit workers, have not been represented in these terms.

By closely examining a series of cultural representations about public-sector unions and workers during these debates, we can better understand the logic at work in making attacks on such unions so widely resonant. Producerism, long associated with whiteness and masculinity, has stood in contrast to parasitism, expressed most visibly through representations of people of color as dependent and self-indulgent. In the cultural representations we examine, opponents of public-sector workers have attempted to transpose the script of parasitism onto workers that have historically been exempt from such charges. Claims that public-sector unions and workers are parasitic on the body politic are only cognizable because of this history of racialized populism. They serve here to enlarge the population of workers and subjects who no longer have an automatic claim on the social wage.

To be clear, we do not argue that white public-sector workers are losing their whiteness in an embodied sense, or that these examples suggest that race is declining in social and political significance. White privilege and white supremacy continue to be powerful, dynamic forces in U.S. political culture, structuring life opportunities, vulnerability to violence and death, and differential access to power.[23] These examples do not suggest that white workers are facing discrimination on the basis of race. Nor do these confrontations with white workers suggest that long-standing racialized political appeals are subsiding. Walker, for example, built much of his electoral base through such appeals to white suburban and rural areas of Wisconsin.[24] We posit instead that the continued upward redistribution of wealth and state power that has accelerated since the Great Recession has lessened the economic guarantees and privileges that many white workers once took for granted. Discourses that long protected many white workers from such charges of parasitism and dependence are open to new deployments and articulations.

Defining Populist Producerism

The framing of public-sector workers and unions as parasitic on taxpayers rests on a long-standing discursive distinction between society's "makers and takers," to borrow a phrase made popular by Mitt Romney's 2012 presidential campaign.[25] Its success depends on the premise that populist politics—and the producerist ideology at its heart—flow from identifiable grievances by those who produce society's wealth against those who consume it without giving back. This "producer ethic," as Alexander Saxton called it, has roots in the Jeffersonian belief that the yeoman farmer, as neither a master nor a slave, was the proper subject of civic virtue, republican liberty, and self-rule. But it first emerged as a broad partisan identity in the antebellum era, where it expressed in the Democratic Party an opposition between white labor and those who would exploit it.[26] Producerist ideology posited not an opposition between workers and owners but a masculine, cross-class assemblage connecting factions of the elite with poor whites both in cities and on the frontier in what Democratic Missouri senator Thomas Hart Benton called "the productive and burthen-bearing classes" in opposition to those cast as unproductive and threatening, including bankers and speculators, slaves, and indigenous people. As such, producerism provided a template for subsequent political intersections of whiteness, masculinity, and labor that would include different groups and target different foes, but was always secured by a logic that described a fundamental division in society between those who create society through their efforts and those who are parasitic on, or destructive of, those efforts.

The division between producer and parasite, it should be stressed, does not correlate with production and nonproduction in any objective sense. The slaveowner was a celebrated element of the Jacksonian coalition, for example, while various forms of slave, contract, or dispossessed labor were reviled. In other words, one's politics do not flow from one's position as a producer. Rather, the very notion of producerism is generated by politics.

In various iterations, producerism has played a central role in U.S. political history. The People's Party of the 1890s invoked the moral status of agricultural and industrial labor against Eastern financial elites. The famed labor anthem of the Industrial Workers of the World, "Solidarity Forever," penned by Ralph Chaplin in 1915, includes the lines, "Is there aught we hold in common with the greedy parasite / Who would lash us into serfdom and would crush us with his might?"[27] During the Great Depression it was the "economic royalists," as President Franklin Roosevelt called them, who were seen to cause the economic crisis, with unions regarded as defenders of the public good. And other critics have pointed out that settler-colonial societies like the United States are by their nature parasitic. As J. Sakai has argued in *Settlers: The Mythology of the White Proletariat*: "The myth of the self-sufficient, white settler family 'clearing the wilderness' and supporting themselves through their own initiative and hard labor, is a propaganda fabrication. It is the absolute characteristic of settler society to be parasitic, dependent upon the superexploitation of oppressed peoples for its style of life. Never has Euro-Amerikan society completely supported itself."[28]

Since the 1960s, however, it is the political right that has most often made populist appeals to producerism. Against the perceived racial liberalism of the mid-1960s, Alabama governor George Wallace and others like him forged a politics that expressed populism in terms at once racist and anti-government, contrasting "pointy-headed bureaucrats" and social engineers to "this man in the textile mill, this man in the steel mill, this beautician" in rants against busing, welfare, crime, and civil rights protest. In 1969, President Richard Nixon began using the terms "Silent Majority," "forgotten Americans," and "Middle America" to describe an aggrieved white majority squeezed by the unruly, dependent poor on one side and government elites on the other. Conservatives stoked political identity across the 1970s in blaming both government and the poor for the victimization of taxpayers and the moral decline of the country.[29]

Numerous liberal writers, including Thomas and Mary Edsall and Todd Gitlin, have lamented this shift in populism from left to right.[30] For them, the natural political identity of workers and farmers expressed in opposition to monopoly capitalists, bankers, and speculators was relinquished to the right as the moral language of labor was replaced with excessive concern for identity—be it race, nationality, gender, or sexuality—fragmenting a coherent left identity. Such an understanding fails in two ways, however. First, identity has always been central to populism insofar as it has expressed whiteness and masculinity as central features of who is included in populist rhetoric. Second, a simple story of a rightward shift misses the ways in which, from the Jacksonian era forward, producerist politics have always retained elements of racialized demonization, be it the anti-Black and anti-indigenous politics of the Jacksonians, the anti-Chinese campaigns of white labor in the 1880s, the anti-immigrant sentiment in the early twentieth century, or the exclusion of Black workers from New Deal programs.

Populist identity distinguishes itself not just against those seen as exploitive elites above and parasitic dependents below but also against elements in society depicted as imprudent, excessive, wasteful, and indolent. Nineteenth-century minstrel shows, for instance, portrayed Black people not merely as lazy but also as sexually promiscuous, voracious, and frolicsome. As David Roediger, Eric Lott, and Michael Rogin have all demonstrated, part of minstrelsy's appeal was in identification and desire as much as in demonization and abjection. White workers under the yoke of industrial discipline and Victorian morality in the nineteenth century were drawn to the stage shows of blacked-up whites performing songs and skits that were playfully erotic, that lampooned elites, and that celebrated the avoidance of work. Yet blackface served to resecure the boundaries of white, bourgeois morality by serving as an exaggerated symbol of what had to be rejected by the producerist ethic, while stoking envy and rage against actual people of color.[31]

The deep logic of producerism thus structures representations of its negation, the parasite, which since the 1960s in particular has been constructed in highly racialized and gendered terms—the mother on welfare, an immigrant draining public coffers, the criminal "coddled" by liberal judges, or the undeserving recipient of affirmative action. These scripts animate the attack on public-sector unions and workers, continually contrasting its version of the producer—in this case the taxpayer and private-sector worker—with public unions and workers. As we demonstrate, these workers are depicted as unproductive, wasteful, excessive, and indolent; they indulge in the envied pleasures of shorter working hours, long vacations, and early retirement. They are cognizable precisely because they invoke a longer genealogy of the discourse of racial parasitism and producerism, and its representation of fiscal burdens. Framed this way, unionized public-sector workers become threats to taxpayers—not merely economically but socially and psychologically as well.

Key to the successful development of populist anti-statism has been its selective, racial deployment, avoiding discussion of forms of state authority and distribution that have been enjoyed by the great majority of the white electorate since the New Deal, such as Social Security, Medicare, and government-secured home loans. Attacks on the state from the right were aimed originally at school desegregation after the *Brown v. Board of Education* decisions, and later busing, fair housing, anti-discrimination law, and affirmative action; and in response to programs seen to favor poor people of color, such as Aid to Families with Dependent Children and Medicaid. Conservatives extended this strategy by targeting other figures of racial vulnerability, such as immigrant children in public schools.[32]

At each stage of the development of anti-statism, a racialized line separating the deserving from the undeserving was drawn to bolster its claims. Now, the logic of anti-statism has become so pervasive, and its success against everything from busing to affirmative action to welfare so thorough, that advocates have begun to turn it against new targets. Political elements made vulnerable in class terms can now be attacked via racial logic. The line between the deserving and undeserving has been moved such that a large number of white workers now fall on the latter side of the line as "takers."[33]

This transformation is rooted in a generation of neoliberal economic restructuring, as cuts in income-transfer payments and reductions in property, income, and capital gains taxes shifted more of the responsibility for funding public services from corporations and the wealthy onto middle- and low-income workers. Households faced with flattening wages and rising levels of debt increasingly came to demand tax relief of their own as a way to safeguard their income, giving rise to a populist tax revolt. In this context, the public sector itself became stigmatized as a drain on the budgets of ordinary workers rather than as a keystone of social equity and income security and mobility. As a result, a broad range of income-transfer programs, including welfare, assistance to immigrants, and other public-health, education, and employment initiatives, became defunded, most often by the attacking of their beneficiaries as undeserving and parasitic.[34]

The financial crisis of 2008 represented a culmination of these developments. For many years, revenue-starved states and municipalities that were unable to offer meaningful wage increases to their employees instead promised expanded retirement and health benefits to such workers that were less straining to their budgets in the short run. But as government revenues plummeted after the housing and banking crisis, and with most other income-transfer programs already eviscerated, public-sector workers and their benefits became subject to new political scrutiny. The number of public-sector jobs declined significantly after the Great Recession; in 2018, the proportion of state and local employees in the civilian workforce was at its lowest level since 1967.[35]

Public-sector employment has historically been an important source of economic mobility for women and people of color. In regions with large numbers of unionized public-sector workers, such as New York City, unionization substantially decreases race and gender pay disparities as a whole. Public-sector job losses during the Great Recession thus had a disproportionate impact on women workers and Black workers.[36] According to the Economic Policy Institute, from 2007 to 2011 roughly 765,000 jobs were cut in state and local governments. Women held seven in ten of those jobs, and African Americans held two in ten.[37] The sociologist Jennifer Laird points out that Black women become doubly disadvantaged under these conditions as they are overrepresented in a shrinking area of the economy while facing higher barriers to finding private-sector employment.[38]

Nationally, however, Black public-sector workers are unionized at slightly lower rates than non-Black workers. To make public-sector workers the focus of public opprobrium, attacks could not single out workers of color alone, nor could they simply focus on structural or political critiques of unions. Instead, as we explore below, the claims turned on the alleged greed, excess, and moral failures of workers themselves, including white workers. The scripts of parasitism that have long justified the subordination of people of color have become available to stigmatize and represent some white workers to justify their exclusion from the social wage.

Parasitism as Gluttony

In order to fully understand the logic of the attack on public-sector unions, we need to comprehend the ways in which the identity of the productive, taxpaying citizen is brought into being and continually defended against threats to its integrity. This integrity, we argue, is economic, moral, and even bodily. Unions and government workers are represented as wasteful, excessive, festive, and grotesque threats to an independent, virtuous, sober, frugal subject.[39] These qualities, evoking both envy and disgust, transform public-sector workers from productive citizens into social threats—not merely to public budgets but to the social order itself.

Cultural representations such as the editorial cartoons examined below are important forms of evidence, not because they permit claims about causality but rather because they express the political claims we analyze by casting into sharp relief the charges of parasitism, laziness, gluttony and destructiveness of the public-sector worker on behalf of the beleaguered host—the taxpaying citizen. Cartoons evoke visceral responses—laughter, disgust, outrage—to a political point the cartoonist seeks to make. The intended meanings of political cartoons are generally self-evident, which allows the analyst to focus on how the cartoon achieves its intended effect. Cartoons, which can be absorbed and understood quickly by readers, often enjoy broad circulation—particularly those in syndication. They act as snapshots—moments of temporarily fixed understandings of a political phenomenon.

For our argument, cartoons are an especially salient form of evidence. The contemporary attacks on public-sector workers we analyze dispense with claims about the political power of public unions over government functions or their likelihood of pulling electoral politics leftward, as was the case in conservative attacks on public unions in prior decades. The accusations leveled at these unions today depend less on sophisticated institutional and ideological arguments and more on the visceral description of indolence on the one hand and rapacity on the other, thus extending their appeal across previously established ideological boundaries.

To take one example, anti-union editorial cartoons commonly depict public-sector workers as massive entities—voracious, grotesquely fat, and even cannibalistic—in contrast to the diminutive taxpayer, often portrayed as "the little guy," who is threatened, bullied, or simply overmatched. Such depictions demonstrate that it is not enough merely to present unions as politically and economically powerful. Obesity and cannibalism evoke deeper bodily fears and forms of abjection—threatening the very corporeal integrity of the subject. In these portrayals we also see the racial transposition in action. Racialized bodies, which underscore the cultural framing of unions, come to signify public-sector workers more generally.

Portrayals of unions as voracious destroyers circulated widely during the Chicago Teacher Union's (CTU) strike in September 2012, directed in particular against union president Karen Lewis. During the nearly two-week strike, Lewis became the CTU's most visible public figure not only in pressing for improvements in pay, working conditions, and job security but also in more broadly resisting the efforts of Mayor Rahm Emanuel to close dozens of schools and to reduce public control over the school system.[40] We begin with an examination of depictions of Lewis, because she is both emblematic of public unions *and* Black. The logic of racial transposition, as we have argued, is that historic forms of anti-Blackness provide the template for attacking largely white targets. We can see how portrayals of Lewis rely on well-worn popular depictions of Black people in general and Black women in particular. Those same tropes appear in treatments of public-sector unions more generally.

Editorial cartoons during the strike consistently represented Lewis's body as corpulent and insatiable. One cartoon by Lisa Benson syndicated by the *Washington Post* depicts Lewis shouting through a bullhorn, "WHAT DO WE WANT? WE WANT MORE!!" Lewis is shown standing on the back of a white man wearing a Cubs baseball cap and holding a sign that says "BROKE! Please Help!"[41] Here Lewis, signifying the irrational, rapacious demands of the CTU and Chicago public-school teachers, is literally breaking the back of a helpless white Chicagoan.

An exemplary depiction was featured on the conservative blog site *Chicago News Bench*. It is a manipulation of a photo to depict Lewis as extraordinarily obese, holding a plate carrying a baby's head. The caption reads, "Chicago Teacher's Union President Karen Lewis wants to eat your children. With cheese and bacon."[42] The accompanying article reads in part: "This fat pig of a union bully doesn't give a damn about the kids in the Chicago Public Schools

"What Do We Want? We Want More!!" Lisa Benson, editorial cartoon, September 9, 2012, reprinted with permission from Lisa Benson, the Washington Post Writers Group, and the Cartoonist Group. All rights reserved.

(CPS). She doesn't care about their parents, either, many of whom had to scramble today to make arrangements for safety of their children." We include it here less because of the image's circulation— its intended audience is specifically Chicago-area conservatives— but rather because it so clearly elucidates the political–cultural appeal we describe.

While orality and associations with cannibalism were staples of blackface minstrelsy, they can also be elements of political signification more generally. As the political theorist Anne Norton has demonstrated in her work on political identity, "eating provides names and explanatory metaphors for relations of power."[43] Oral aggression, associated gluttony, and even cannibalism turn up repeatedly in depictions of public unions. The conservative columnist Michelle Malkin referred to Lewis as "Chicago thuggery personified" and a "union fat cat."[44] The online news site *Chicago News Report*, describing a talk Lewis gave at the Northwest

Teaching for Social Justice Conference in Seattle in 2011, said that she was "apparently . . . possessed by the ghost of Moms Mabley" and that it was as if "an evil, comedic spirit had taken control of her mouth," because of comments she made about Education Secretary Arne Duncan.[45]

Comments posted to a YouTube clip of that talk are instructive. One poster, directly making the link between bodily and professional discipline, wrote, "Well it's tough to take someone seriously when they lack the self-control and discipline to manage their own health. It shows lack of character." Another post links oral aggression to her role as Teacher's Union official: "That's not a woman, that's a theme park—or a woman that ate a theme park. Her navel's probably large enough to accomodate [sic] another classroom for 20 or more students." A more explicit post links race hatred, weight, and cannibalism: "na na na na niiiiig can you imagine this woman teaching kids. I'd be fearful of her eating them." Or quite directly: "WHY IS THIS GROTESQUE THE STEWARD OF AMERICA'S CHILDREN?"[46]

Anonymous web postings such as these reveal the affective logic at work, as they allow their authors direct, uncensored expression. Here, a representative of a strong public-sector union is described in ways that show us how the producer is constituted as white, hardworking, virtuous, and threatened by the insatiability of public unions.

The associative links between Blackness, excess, and orality demonstrate the substratum of producerist identity in the examples above. But what is peculiar to this historical moment is the mobilization of producerism against political elements not directly associated with people of color. Indeed, the attack on public-sector unions requires a rhetoric that can cast white workers—once the unquestioned subjects of producerism—as parasitic outsiders. Accomplishing this identity shift has required a transformation of unions into grotesques.

Another cartoon from spring 2010 by syndicated cartoonist Sean Delonas, who had previously been accused of racism for a *New York Post* cartoon implying that Obama was a chimpanzee,[47] appeared in the conservative *City Journal* accompanying an article titled "The Beholden State: How Public Unions Broke California." Here, public unions are represented by an enormous pig—an animal symbolically associated with gluttony and filth—eating pizza, an ice cream cone, and a soda, telling a skeletal corpse representing the California taxpayer: "You're just going to have to tighten your belt."[48] In this representation, public unions eat up resources needed to sustain life. It should be noted that what has been starved here is not the people of California but rather the *individual* taxpayer. In other words, the collective threatens to destroy the individual.

In another cartoon, this one by the popular syndicated cartoonist Mike Lester, the union does not merely devour public funds and thereby starve the taxpayer, but rather engages in direct cannibalism. The illustration depicts a "Gov. union worker" saying, "This is what democra-(urp!!)cy looks like" as he consumes the head of a proportionately miniature taxpayer.[49] Lester's cartoon, published at the height of the mass demonstrations at the Wisconsin state capitol in the winter of 2011, turns democratic contestation into oral aggression.

In both cartoons, eating underscores the fear of the destructive power of unions. It should also be noted that in these cartoons, the gluttonous union is a *collective* entity that destroys the *individual* taxpayer. Here, racial transposition occurs through use of the racialized discourse of aggressive parasitism as it is directed against white workers as well as Black. This is achieved affectively through the transfer and expansion of racial notions of orality and corpulence to a broader category of workers.

Parasitism as Idleness

A second important dimension in the discourse of parasitism emphasizes idleness and indolence, traits long used to justify the subordination of Black and brown laboring bodies. These themes are repurposed in recent representations of public-sector workers, who are similarly depicted as antithetical to the virtuous producer. Again, analyzing representations of these themes in popular culture reveals the particular logic through which they are constructed and made legible to wider publics.

In an April 2010 *Saturday Night Live* award-show parody skit titled "2010 Public Employee of the Year," guest host Gabourey Sidibe (star of the 2009 film *Precious*) is cast as a St. Louis Department of Motor Vehicles employee named "Markeesha Odom." Odom is the first to be introduced as a finalist for the award. The narrator explains she has been "twice named Missouri's 'Surliest and Least Cooperative' state employee"; Sidibe scowls at the camera, hand on hip, lips pursed. Sidibe is then congratulated for working at a DMV facility with twenty-four employees who "went through an entire day without helping a single customer."

SNL cast thirty-three-year-old Kenan Thompson, one of only two Black ensemble members, to play the award show's host, "Desmond McCoy," an Oakland bus driver and union member who retired on full benefits because of (clearly fraudulent) "job related stress." Thompson's character explains facetiously: "In these times of anti-tax hysteria and threats of government budget cuts, it's important to remember that people with government jobs are like workers everywhere. Except for lifetime job security, guaranteed annual raises, early retirement on generous pensions and full medical coverage with no deductibles and office visit fees or co-payments."[50]

The script of parasitism and dependence is made visible through familiar performances of race and gender. Thompson is cast as a hustler, naturally seeking to get around a hard day's work for his own gratification. Sidibe's character is cast in a classic "Sapphire" role, represented in countless popular culture narratives as "evil, bitchy, stubborn and hateful," and frames and performs the producer-versus-parasite distinction in this context.[51] Her character rehearses long-standing racist portrayals of Black women as slothful and belligerent that continue to pervade television and other media forms in the United States. Sidibe's and Thompson's characters are immediately legible in the context of these well-worn scripts; as the theorist M. Jaqui Alexander explains, they are "culturally legitimate to despise."[52]

The two other "finalists" for the "Public Employee of the Year" award are cast as white men—one a janitor, the other an elevator

Still from 2010 Public Employee of the Year skit, *Saturday Night Live*, "Gabourey Sidibe."
Left to right: Bobby Moynihan, Jason Sudeikis, Gabourey Sidibe. Season 35, episode 20, April 24, 2010. Photograph by Dana Edelson/NBC/NBCU Photo Bank via Getty Images.

inspector. Both revel in do-nothing government jobs, limitless over-time, and farcical work rules secured by a union contract. Here, the viewers are introduced to the logic of parasitism through a Black woman, a logic that becomes transposed to two white male characters and is recognizable in part through their association with Sidibe's character. Indeed, the skit would not function the same way if the men were introduced first; their dependence and parasitism could not be naturally assumed by viewers. The process of transposition, we should note, does not erase or trouble the boundaries of their social identities. The race and gendered performances delimit the characters and their social distance from one another in clear ways. The two male characters are hopelessly parasitic, but they have not lost or sacrificed their whiteness in any way. They are parasitic and they are white.

Americans for Prosperity (AFP), a Tea Party–aligned political advocacy group that has spearheaded the assault on public-sector unions through many of its state and local chapters, has also been on the forefront of attempts to portray public workers as anti-producers, indolent and idle. Their efforts reveal the kinds of labor necessary to put white workers in this category. In 2011, AFP California produced a series of online videos called *Lifestyles of the Rich and Infamous on Government Pensions,* featuring AFP spokesperson David Spady clad in a tuxedo and driving to different locales (sometimes in a stretch limousine) to highlight the allegedly excessive compensation and benefits commanded by specific public-sector workers.[53] (The segment spoofs *Lifestyles of the Rich and Famous*, a syndicated show from the 1980s in which the host, Robin Leech, toured the homes and locales of entertainment stars.)

One AFP segment targeted municipal lifeguards in Newport Beach, California, as an example not only of the excessive pay and benefits afforded to public workers at taxpayer expense but also of the self-gratifying and indulgent nature of the workers themselves. AFP California complained that Newport lifeguards were overcompensated through high salaries, excessive pensions, and early retirement plans that impoverished taxpayers. The producerist discourse of recent decades does not easily lend itself to the demonization of white male rescue workers, particularly after the lionization of "first responders" in the wake of September 11. In some cases, the pensions of firefighters and police officers have generated political controversy, but those criticisms never focused on personal qualities or attributes as such. But lifeguards are more vulnerable to the logics of both producerism and austerity, occupying a more liminal category and therefore standing as an appealing target.

In order to make their case compelling, AFP depicts lifeguards as frivolous, vain, and focused on the pleasures of the body, characteristics that are in opposition to the masculinist logic of producerism and are an affront to the demand for austerity. These elements of producerist discourse, part and parcel of the depictions of women and people of color in contrast to virtuous white men, are now meant to mark certain white male subjects off from others who are more immune to attack.

Attempts at new discursive framings do not necessarily succeed. In this case, however, the notion of the lifeguard as a decadent threat to the polity was understandable enough to cross over to popular media presentation. The syndicated television news program *Inside Edition* embraced AFP's framing by running an "investigative" segment on the lifeguards, in which Spady appears as a "whistleblower" who exposes the corrupt practices of the municipal lifeguards, highlighting vanity and sexual pleasure seeking alongside overcompensation. In an interview on the *Inside Edition* segment, Spady complains that "the reason lifeguards have some of the most coveted jobs in Southern California is not just because they get to talk to girls in bikinis and work on their suntans" but because of the "incredibly generous packages" they are afforded. To see if taxpayers are "getting their money's worth," *Inside Edition* producers and a reporter secretly followed several lifeguards over several days, filming them playing beach volleyball and running errands, allegedly on work time. A reporter confronts one lifeguard supervisor in his car in a parking lot (after reportedly following him four hundred miles to the San Francisco Bay Area), asking him, "Do you think you owe an explanation to the taxpayers who pay your salary?" Though later in the segment the reporter discloses a seemingly reasonable explanation given by the city manager for all of the alleged infractions, the underlying contention was clear—preening, hedonistic lifeguards were now fleecing taxpayers too. A cultural narrative rarely deployed against white workers was easily understood in this context; once they are framed as parasites and as threats to the producerist public, neither whiteness nor masculinity could indemnify the lifeguards from these charges.[54]

The AFP story garnered significant press coverage in Orange County, and in early 2014 the City of Newport announced it was seeking bids from private contractors to outsource some lifeguarding services, citing the need to control pension and salary costs. While municipal pensions have been an ongoing source of debate in many California cities, it is the way in which the cultural logic of parasitism and self-indulgence becomes visible in public debate here that requires our attention.[55]

Reclaiming the (White) Producerist Subject

We have argued that in order to understand why public-employee unions quickly became an object of bipartisan opprobrium during the Great Recession, we must attend to the cultural logics and representational strategies that opponents of such unions sought to popularize. Opponents of public-sector unions transposed narratives long used to stigmatize people of color and to discredit state redistributory efforts to improve their conditions onto a largely white workforce, portraying government workers as decadent and slothful threats to the productive, taxpaying citizenry, legitimating and naturalizing a series of anti-union policy initiatives in several states.

Like all articulatory projects, however, the claims they made and the identities and interests they sought to naturalize are always contingent and incomplete. More particularly, public-sector unions and their supporters have played an active role in challenging representations of public-sector workers as parasitic. But rather than challenge the cultural logic of parasitism, they largely claimed the producerist position for themselves in order to discredit these attacks.

This strategy can be witnessed most visibly in the successful 2011 campaign on the part of public-sector workers in Ohio to reverse the passage of Senate Bill (SB) 5, a law backed by Republican governor John Kasich that dramatically curtailed the rights and power of the state's 360,000 public workers. SB 5 banned strikes by all public-sector workers, restricted collective bargaining to a handful of issues, eliminated binding arbitration, banned unions from collecting "fair share" fees to cover the costs of representing employees included in the collective bargaining agreement who elected not to pay membership dues, restricted other pay and benefits, and increased the minimum employee contributions toward health-care benefits.[56] Unlike the Wisconsin legislation, the bill also restricted the rights and authority of police and firefighters. After Kasich signed the legislation into law on March 30, 2011, a coalition of public-sector unions and their supporters organized under the entity "We Are Ohio" (the campaign name itself signifying its populist and producerist commitments) and qualified a statewide referendum on the measure for the fall 2011 ballot, which became known as Issue 2.

In the public debate over the measure, supporters of SB 5 mobilized familiar arguments about union members as parasites. As one television ad in favor of the anti-union measure had it, "Enough is enough." Public-sector workers opposed the legislation, the ad claimed, "because they want even more from us. Better pay and benefits than us. Better job security than us. Better retirement than us. All paid for by us." Republican state legislator Jim Buchy explained that SB 5 was needed because "We want to create more taxpayers and fewer tax users."[57] In an interview with Toledo news station WUPW in late September, Kasich argued that Ohio voters were tired of "paying twice" for their own benefits and those of public-sector workers, suggesting the example of a "single mother with a couple of kids, it's hard for her to get her health care, she probably has no pension or maybe a 401(k), and we're asking her—it's very tough to support her own family—also to support somebody else's [family]."[58]

The campaign to defeat SB 5 raised more than $40 million, more than three times as much as its opposition, and the money permitted the We Are Ohio coalition to invest heavily in television campaign advertisements.[59] The framing of these ads is instructive, for it reveals the racial logic and representational strategies deployed by the unions to counter the claims of parasitism they faced. The large majority of these ads featured firefighters, police officers, and nurses amid life-threatening emergencies, invoking an iconography of white heroism and sacrifice, and within recognizably gendered occupations.

We Are Ohio's credibility with voters depended on the celebrated cultural status of firefighters, police, and nurses as "first responders" rather than as public-service workers defending the public good. For example, one mailer used in the direct-mail campaign to voters featured an image of two mask-clad firefighters entering a building enveloped in fire and smoke. The accompanying text read, "Fire. Crimes. Rescue. They keep our communities safe." Inside, the text read, "TAKE IT FROM THOSE ON THE

FRONT LINES: Issue 2 makes it harder for our fire, police, and emergency forces to protect us and our families." Unions argued that by restricting collective bargaining to wages and benefits alone, firefighters, nurses, and similar workers would not be able to bargain for adequate staffing levels necessary to respond to emergencies.[60]

The statewide television advertising campaign similarly featured a series of rescue workers responding to emergencies. A widely run ad titled "Zoey" showed a photo of firefighters rescuing a young girl (Zoey) from the upper levels of a burning building, while her great-grandmother explained in a voiceover that "if not for the firefighters, we wouldn't have our Zoey today. . . . That's why it is so important to vote no on Issue 2." Another ad, titled "Emergency," showed firefighters rushing out of the station and fighting a house fire, with a fireman explaining, "Issue 2 makes it harder for us to do our jobs, and that's not safe for us, or the neighborhoods we serve." The ad was rolled out during press conferences at several firehouses around the state, with a largely white and all-male group of firefighters gathered behind the podium.[61] Other ads, titled "Everyday Heroes," "Nurse," and "Sacrifice," included similar images of heroic public-safety workers, nurses, and (in one instance) teachers.[62]

We Are Ohio also launched a significant field-organizing campaign that involved many thousands of public-sector union members and their supporters contacting voters at their homes and by phone. On Election Day, Issue 2 lost in a landslide; more than 61 percent of voters rejected the anti-union measure. SB 5 was never implemented, handing Governor Kasich a significant defeat.

To be sure, the campaign strategy pursued by We Are Ohio to defeat Issue 2 was highly persuasive with voters. The decision to feature rescue workers and raise the specter of threats to public safety seemingly resonated with undecided voters, who may not have otherwise been supportive of unions or collective bargaining rights. By all accounts, the campaign was well executed and represented a critical victory for organized labor and their allies in the wake of Governor Scott Walker's anti-union attacks in Wisconsin earlier in the year.

For the purpose of our analysis, what is instructive about these ads and the broader campaign strategy is the terrain on which unions had to make their claims to the public. In the face of charges of parasitism, they had to quite literally perform their white producerist commitments for the electorate, in effect to counter the process of racial transposition.[63] In order to refute accusations that they were burdens to the taxpayer and dependent on other workers, they had to appear as the negation of the parasite, the indispensable and heroic protectors of public safety, affirmed by their whiteness within traditional gender roles. That is, they had to reproduce the long-standing producer/parasite divide (positioning themselves firmly on the side of the former) to legitimate their standing before the electorate.

This strategy was likely necessary to win the election that November, but in the long term it forces public-sector workers in general to operate in an extremely constricted political framework. Many public-employee unions have long been ambivalent about championing the public sector and government more broadly as a means to secure widespread social mobility and justice, choosing more often to serve primarily as bargaining agents to secure better wages and working conditions for their members.[64] In this sense, the emphasis on valorizing white heroism rather than making claims for the public good is not surprising.

But there are tens of thousands of public-sector workers—clerks, accountants, social workers, data analysts, custodians, and many others—who can never be represented in such heroic terms. How do they make their claim to collective bargaining rights, fair wage standards, and health and retirement benefits? If future attacks on public-sector unions are more selective and exempt public-safety workers, on what grounds can other public-sector employees defend themselves? The producer/hero framework may legitimate the claim that only subjects who can perform and document their productive contributions are worthy of public remuneration and benefits, narrowing the terrain on which others can make claims to the public wage. By defending public workers on such terms, it naturalizes and reproduces the producer/parasite distinction.

These conditions also have implications beyond the public sector. As we argued earlier, "producerism" does not correspond to any particular position or role in the economy; it is a socially determined identity. For example, workers in electronics assembly, meat processing, or garment factories, where large numbers of women, immigrants, and people of color are concentrated, are centrally involved in the manufacture of goods. Yet they rarely stand in for the producerist ethic, and the logic of producerism has not been mobilized to protect their vulnerability. When politicians want to demonstrate their commitments to producerism and "American jobs," they are much more likely to visit a heavy-manufacturing plant in the Midwest than a sweatshop in downtown Los Angeles. Thus, the most culturally legible forms of producerism are always constrained by racial and gender conventions. And even for those white workers who do imagine that producerist logics will safeguard their employment and wages from attacks, the example of public-sector workers is instructive. Within a cultural discourse and policy framework that fetishizes and naturalizes market forces, anyone perceived to have job security, wages, benefits, or even the most basic forms of autonomy and authority at work can stand accused of violating the ethical norms of producerism. And as the sectors of the economy long associated with producerism continue to shrink, the protections of claims to a producerist identity will also wither.

Moreover, invocations of producerism will always deny and occlude the ongoing dependence and parasitism of a settler-colonial nation itself. Any invocation of an innocent and virtuous producer in this context necessarily obscures these relations of theft and the production of social death that have constituted the nation's development and mode of governance since the arrival of European settlers. In this context, there are no self-sufficient subjects. Producerism is also the last refuge of scoundrels. As the Ohio example demonstrates, labor-union producerism will almost always be articulated through the dominant conventions of race, gender, and nation. The "Buy American" campaigns pushed by organized labor in the 1970s and 1980s were rife with racist suppositions about the inscrutability of "foreign" labor seeking to depose the virtuous

American worker. Such laborist appeals to producerism not only amplified nativist sentiments (and anti-immigrant violence) but also failed to prevent corporations from driving down wages globally by shifting production to sites with lower labor costs.[65]

Beyond the Producer/Parasite Divide

In the wake of the defeat of Issue 2 and the considerable political backlash against Scott Walker, many of the attacks on public-sector unions moved to the legal arena. The U.S. Supreme Court heard several cases to determine whether workers included in collective bargaining agreements can be compelled to pay fees to cover the cost of their representation.[66] By 2012, the contention that unionized public-sector workers were one of the primary culprits of the Great Recession seemed to have less resonance. In November 2012, voters decisively rejected a measure to weaken the political power of unions in California. "Right-to-work" initiatives failed to qualify for the ballot in Ohio and Oregon the same year.

While organized conservative interests continue to press their case against public-sector workers, and many states and municipalities continue to debate pension funding in particular, cultural representations of public-sector workers as parasitic lessened, but they did not altogether disappear.[67] In early 2018, public school teachers in Oklahoma joined colleagues in West Virginia, Kentucky, and Arizona in statewide walkouts to demand both pay increases for themselves and more funding for K–12 education. Teachers in Oklahoma had not received a pay raise in a decade, and the state ranked last in teacher salaries. Many school systems, even in white middle-class communities, were chronically underfunded.

The walkout raised the ire of some fiscal conservatives, especially as teachers continued to press their case even after the legislature granted an increase to the K–12 budget that would provide for modest raises. Oklahoma state senator Joseph Silk turned to a familiar script to frame the walkouts as threats to the producerist body. Silk commented on Facebook that he was "exceptionally frustrated with many of our public educators, who radically and vocally turned against all common sense, principled measures, measures which could have increased funding to their industry and instead threw all their support behind a huge money grab tax increase on the backs of hard working Oklahomans."[68] Two weeks later, when Kentucky governor Matt Bevin was met by five thousand teachers descending on the state capitol to protest funding cuts and stagnant salaries, he attacked them for "hangin' out, shoes off. Smokin', leavin' trash around, takin' the day off."[69] For Bevin, the teachers were unmistakably parasites, unworthy of public sympathy and support.

These changing but enduring representations demonstrate the contingency and fluidity of the process by which certain political subjects are marked as either productive or parasitic. While populist charges of parasitism have historically been made on groups marked racially as non-white, white workers can also be subject to the logic of this framework through a process of racial transposition. Though the fiscal crises engendered by the Great Recession undoubtedly made the attacks on public-sector workers more resonant, economic conditions alone do not explain their sudden emergence. Instead, the discourse of parasitism, so historically significant in U.S. political culture, allowed these attacks to be read as reasonable, prudent responses to a population thriving off the labor of others.

Yet this paradigm is not inevitable. Some recent public-sector organizing efforts have effectively made their demands and claims legible without reproducing the claims of producerism. The 2012 citywide strike led by the Chicago Teachers Union effectively aligned the needs of teachers, parents, students, and working-class neighborhoods without asserting the uncompromised virtue or needs of one group against another. (By contrast, the charter school and education privatization movements explicitly pit needy parents and students against allegedly greedy teachers and their unions.) The strike won important benefits for teachers and protections and resources for neighborhood schools.[70] In West Virginia six years later, teachers, bus drivers, and other school employees struck in all fifty-five counties statewide; thirty-four thousand teachers, with the support of hundreds of thousands of parents, closed every school in the state. The strike forced the legislature to contribute hundreds of millions of dollars to the school budget without making cuts to other public services. As with similar education strikes in Kentucky, Arizona, and Oklahoma, the demands in West Virginia were premised on meeting broad-based public needs and confronting the logic of austerity rather than celebrating the producerist qualities of any single group.[71]

Teacher-led organizing in West Virginia, Oklahoma, and Arizona has been dubbed by some commentators as the "red-state revolt."[72] These actions certainly confound simplistic accounts of place-based political cultures (blue versus red) offered by observers like Thomas Edsall and Amy Chua, who suggest that competing political "tribes" marked by clashing ideological commitments structure the contours of political antagonisms in the United States.[73] Yet as we will see in the next chapter, the discourse of racialized producerism continues to perform important ideological labor in the New Gilded Age. Critical race scholars have long asserted that "race" is a social and political construct. Taking that claim seriously means not simply marking the ways racial discourse travels along well-trodden paths of ascription. Insofar as race is the product of power, we should attend to ways race can be mobilized to surprising ends, pressed into service to shore up or extend hierarchy and domination. Thus we should expect the discourse of parasitism to continue to incorporate new subjects, interests, and political projects in the future, particularly in the absence of more fundamental challenges to its logic. As long as this framework remains resonant, all workers are vulnerable to its imperatives.

2

"THE INCOMPREHENSIBLE MALICE—
OF POOR WHITE AMERICA"

New Racializations of White Precarity

• • •

The continued upward redistribution of wealth that has accelerated since the Great Recession has greatly reduced the economic
guarantees and privileges that many white Americans once took
for granted. This period marks the longest span since the New
Deal that many white households have experienced sustained economic abandonment—facing levels of debt, impoverishment, and
vulnerability that historically only existed in particular regions or
economic sectors. Even since the recovery began in 2009, some 95
percent of the country's income gains went to households in the
top 1 percent. To be clear, Black workers, low-wage immigrants,
and other low-income households of color fared far worse in this
era. Median household wealth for white families in 2015 remained
twelve times higher than for Black families, and wealth accumulation in Black and Latino/a households has declined steadily in
the last thirty years; households headed by women of color face
even sharper disparities.[1] But due to enormous income and wealth
expansion among the top 5 percent of white households, these
median figures also mask the stagnation and decline in wealth and
wages for white households in the bottom 50 percent of earners.
For many whites, their racial positioning and privilege has not
indemnified them from these transformations.

This chapter explores the contradictory ways in which white
political identity becomes mobilized, inhabited, contested, and

transformed in the context of material crisis and abandonment. What happens when both the material and "public and psychological wage" of whiteness famously described by W. E. B. Du Bois is no longer paid out as it was throughout much of the postwar era?[2] What political subjectivities and projects are made possible and likely under these conditions? And how do political elites in general and conservatives in particular, who have come to power since the late 1960s, explain the greater precarity faced by the significant numbers of middle- and working-class whites who helped put them in office?

The Declining Public Investment in Whiteness

Before the New Deal, being recognized as white secured some social and political privileges but few economic guarantees. The social insurance programs originating from the New Deal in the 1930s and 1940s changed all that.[3] Massive federal, state, and local commitments to agricultural subsidies, investments in public infrastructure (especially electrification and transportation), labor policy (collective bargaining rights and unemployment insurance), pensions and social security, and housing and education subsidies lifted millions of households out of poverty. These investments also attached a particular material basis to the ways in which whiteness functioned as a signifier of social privilege and status. And while billions of public dollars were redistributed to white low- to middle-income male-headed households, the various forms this public support took were never stigmatized as dependency or parasitism. White workers could thus enjoy enormous public benefits allocated on a racially discriminatory basis, such as government-subsidized home loans, mortgage interest deductions, tuition subsidies, unemployment insurance, social security benefits, and investments in infrastructure programs including freeways and suburbanization projects, while still imagining their economic mobility and social well-being as products of their own work ethic and achievement.[4] Indeed, these guarantees were themselves part of the transformation into an unquestioned whiteness for southern and eastern Europeans, Jews, Slavs, and other immigrant populations from the first Great Wave of immigration from 1880 to 1924.[5]

As the legal theorist Cheryl Harris has demonstrated, the state served to imbue white racial status as a form of "treasured property" premised directly on the power to exclude. To identify as white was to inhabit and embrace a "settled expectation" of this relative status and privilege ensured by the state. As Harris explains: "Becoming white meant gaining access to a whole set of public and private privileges that materially and permanently guaranteed basic subsistence needs, and therefore, survival. Becoming white increased the possibility of controlling critical aspects of one's life rather than being the object of others' domination."[6]

Joel Olson notes that these benefits were provided in large part in order to bind a large section of wage workers to the interests of elites. "The American racial order," he explains, "has historically been constituted by a cross-class alliance between capital and a section of the working class. White is the term for members of this alliance."[7] Olson, building on the work of Du Bois and others, describes whiteness in this way as a "form of social status" or a "standing" that provided a "glass floor below which the white citizen could see but never fall."[8] Importantly, during the period of slavery, indigenous land dispossession, and Jim Crow, "white standing was reproduced through the explicit or tacit consent of local, state, and federal governments."[9]

These protections did not preserve the standing of everyone regarded as white equally. As Keeanga-Yamahtta Taylor has it, "'White supremacy' as the official political ideology of the old postbellum southern aristocracy was a political strategy intended to mute the dramatic class differences between rich Southern white men and poor white men. It was never intended that all white men would be 'supreme,' but the Southern white ruling class was mitigating against the potential of Black and white solidarity at the bottom by creating a racial and social hierarchy."[10] The protections of whiteness thus facilitated differential forms of exploitation and abandonment not only for non-white workers but for many whites as well. The political scientist Tiffany Willoughby-Herard observes that "Black people and poor white people are not parallel social locations, even though they are constituted by interested parties and forces claiming to advocate on behalf of white citizens, workers and women."[11] Thus, James Baldwin contends that these forms of cross-class white racial identifications were themselves a form of misrecognition. The white "American delusion," he explained, "is not only that their brothers all are white but that the whites are all their brothers."[12]

In addition, the security and indemnification from vulnerability conferred by whiteness during this period was uneven and never universal. Particularly in rural areas where economies were predicated on resource extraction necessary for the growth and development of cities, the material privileges of whiteness were far less dependable. In 1964, a twelve-page feature by photographer John Dominis in *Life* magazine titled "The Valley of Poverty" depicted families in former coal-mining towns in the Appalachians in eastern Kentucky facing grinding poverty, sickness, and hunger. "In a lonely valley in eastern Kentucky, in the heart of the mountainous region called Appalachia, live an impoverished people whose plight has long been ignored by affluent America," the author explained. "Their homes are shacks without plumbing or sanitation. Their landscape is a man-made desolation of corrugated hills and hollows laced with polluted streams. The people, themselves—often disease-ridden and unschooled—are without jobs and even without hope."[13]

Robert F. Kennedy would return to the region four years later for a two-day, two-hundred-mile "poverty tour" to assess the impact of the first years of the War on Poverty, calling similar attention to dire conditions of abjection.[14] Part of the voyeurism summoned in the coverage and Kennedy's subsequent tour is tied to a long history of imagining Appalachia as a self-contained cultural world of permanent dysfunction. As the public historian Elizabeth Catte argues, these investments only became more heightened after the 2016 election.[15]

What is important to note, however, about the *Life* coverage, the tour by Kennedy, and similar exposés of white poverty during this period are the ways in which white poverty and destitution were regarded as fully exceptional—an "invisible land," as Michael

Harrington put in his 1962 study *The Other America: Poverty in the United States*. Images of malnourished children in eastern Kentucky brought into sharp relief the basic, commonsense understanding that whiteness was *not* naturally associated with conditions of deep poverty; this is precisely what made Dominis's images and Kennedy's tour so compelling to middle-class white readers. While there were debates about the most effective and appropriate policy solutions that might address these conditions—Sargent Shriver, President Lyndon B. Johnson's main public emissary in the War on Poverty, described the programs as "hand-up, not a handout"—there was general agreement that white poverty was an exceptional condition that could and should be remedied rather than an inevitable expression of deficiency and degradation.[16]

By contrast, we should remember that Gunnar Myrdal's massive 1944 study detailing conditions of Black poverty and subordination was titled *An American Dilemma: The Negro Problem and Modern Democracy*. There was nothing "hidden" or illegible about Black dispossession—indeed, it could take on the generalized form of the already understood "Negro problem." Moreover, it was cast as a "dilemma," suggesting this problem's well-understood intractability. The contrasting registers of white poverty as hidden and aberrant and Black poverty as visible and predictable structured public discourses about material inequality across much of the twentieth century. In 1959 the anthropologist Oscar Lewis coined the term "culture of poverty" in his ethnography *Five Families: Mexican Case Studies in the Culture of Poverty*, a concept further elaborated in Daniel Patrick Moynihan's 1965 *The Negro Family: The Case for National Action*. This contention that racial distinction served as a marker of the behavioral and social dysfunctions (particularly around gender and family formation) that trapped people in poverty shaped welfare and income-support policy throughout the post–World War II era.[17]

The explanation of poverty through racialized constructions of culture and dependence allowed the New Deal political order to become open to Republican appeals in the 1960s as the Democratic Party became more closely associated with Black civil rights. Barry Goldwater built his 1964 presidential campaign partly around the courting of white voters through anti-Black racism and by associating the expansion of civil rights with an attack on popular (white) sovereignty and an enlargement of state power at the expense of (white) freedom and autonomy. Richard Nixon and George Wallace expanded and heightened these claims in their presidential bids in 1968 and 1972. As Joseph Lowndes demonstrated in *From the New Deal to the New Right: Race and the Making of Modern Conservatism*, this cross-class alliance of white workers and business elites took many decades and significant political labor to develop and make coherent. Their interests were not naturally aligned, but across time, through a language developed within the Republican Party to address white working- and middle-class voters as the "Silent Majority," "Middle America," "forgotten Americans," and "Reagan Democrats," a modern conservatism developed that conjoined corporatist and market-based commitments with an assurance that white racial status would protect (most) white subjects from the worst consequences of those markets. In the 1990s, centrist Democrats led by Bill Clinton made similar appeals to "angry white men" and "soccer moms." In all these cases, the parties successfully appealed to white Americans across classes in opposition to both government elites and those constructed as the racialized and dependent poor.

All of these appeals depended upon the economic stability of those white voters, such that those voters would associate economic vulnerability with Black and brown communities in poverty. From this perspective, poverty and destitution were products of cultural dysfunction and failed gender and family norms rather than of structural and market forces. Thus, in 1995, when President Clinton signed a comprehensive welfare-reform law that tore large holes in the social safety net, the great majority of the white populace (and its elected officials) cheered. White racial identity had become so thoroughly associated with autonomy, self-sufficiency, and independence that a public effort premised on making poor households even more vulnerable and insecure was perceived as a defense of white economic autonomy, even as the majority of households receiving such benefits were white.[18]

Again, this strategy was effective as long as enough white voters were economically secure enough to make these appeals resonant. But a broad set of factors fueled by structural transformations has slowly eroded the political standing and material security of an increasing percentage of white middle- and low-income workers. The economic guarantees for white workers within the New Deal order have become increasingly less secure since the 1970s, evident in political attacks on unions, cuts in income-redistribution programs, and a weakening of employment standards that had lifted millions of white workers during the postwar period. A host of other forces, including automation, the predominance of the finance and technological sectors, deregulation, tax cuts, capital mobility and flight, and the diversion of public funds from education and social services to policing and prisons, have made tens of millions of white households newly vulnerable to economic crisis.

Thus the broad racial pact that had been in place since the New Deal, in which the large majority of low- and middle-income workers who identified as white could expect some access to the surplus produced by the national economy, has been restructured. Today the wealth gap between the richest 20 percent and the rest of the country is the widest it has been since the late nineteenth century, with the top one-tenth of 1 percent of Americans worth as much as the bottom 90 percent. More than forty-five million people in the United States live below the official poverty line; nineteen million live in extreme poverty.[19] Race unmistakably structures these dispossessions; historic and contemporary patterns of segregation, land appropriation, and discrimination render people of color much more vulnerable to this upward redistribution of wealth. But in the hollowing out of the broad middle class, whiteness no longer guarantees the same form of material security and even social identity, rendering its future far less stable than its recent past.

It must be emphasized that this dispossession is not the result of discriminatory actions targeting white people on the basis of race. The recent rounds of income stagnation, loss of household wealth, and other forms of economic crisis are not the result of any collective redistribution to non-white groups. Such claims are the fantasy of white-nationalist groups on the right, echoed through claims of "white genocide," but they have no basis in reality. Any aggregate or collective material loss borne by white households is dwarfed by far greater losses among workers of color. Households headed by single women of color often have no net wealth to draw upon in times of crisis.[20]

Yet at the same time, Cheryl Harris's observation that "becoming white increased the possibility of controlling critical aspects of one's life," a maxim that has governed the racialized political economy across most of the twentieth century, seems now to require more context and qualification. Whiteness still operates as a form of "treasured property" for many, and as a kind of collective and possessive investment, as demonstrated by George Lipsitz. But there are today many millions of people whose whiteness no longer indemnifies them, their families, or their communities from crisis.

These developments raise fundamental questions about the labor of race in the current conjuncture. On the one hand, whiteness continues to be associated with a range of advantages across all levels of household income. Even at the lowest income strata, poor white households are less likely to be concentrated in high-poverty neighborhoods as poor Black households; have more access to family assets (including emergency cash) in order to survive the effects of financial hardships, such as job loss or long-term disability; face less discrimination in the job market; and are less vulnerable to police surveillance, arrest, and heavy-handed sentencing policies.[21] On the other hand, these privileges are relative rather than absolute. Whiteness alone does not insulate the twenty-eight million white people living in poverty from the effects of hunger and food insecurity, unemployment and underemployment, the burdens of consumer debt, patchwork access to health care (especially reproductive health) and other public services, or even escaping the violence of mass incarceration.[22] Even with the dramatic racial disparities structuring the criminal justice system, the incarceration rate for white males in 2010 was still higher than the rate for any other nation in the world.[23] Twenty-two percent of white males have been arrested by age eighteen. In a country where an estimated twenty-three million adults have a felony conviction and roughly seventy million people, or about one-third of the adult population, has some sort of criminal record, the protections of whiteness for many are incomplete at best.[24]

Deaths of Despair

The sharpest example of these transformations may lie in the steep increase in the rates of "deaths of despair" among middle-aged white people without a college education. In a 2016 study, Princeton economists Anne Case and Angus Deaton presented longitudinal data showing that while mortality rates among Blacks and Latino/as have continued to fall, they have steadily risen for whites. "In 1999, the mortality rate of white non-Hispanics aged 50–54 with only a high-school degree was 30 percent lower than the mortality rate of blacks in the same age group; by 2015, it was 30 percent higher," they argued. "There are similar crossovers between white and black mortality in all age groups from 25–29 to 60–64." Case and Deaton suggest that a "cumulative disadvantage over life" is driving these increases, registered in a sharp growth in deaths by suicide, drugs and alcohol, poisoning, and chronic liver disease and cirrhosis. They also note an increase among the same group of middle-aged high-school-educated whites in self-reported rates of chronic pain, mental illness, and difficulty socializing.[25] The growth in these mortality rates is concentrated almost entirely in counties scoring the highest on measures of economic distress and among individuals who do not have a college degree. These increases in white mortality are spatially uneven; they have been highest in rural areas outside of the coastal metropolises.[26]

Case and Deaton argue that an "accumulation of pain, distress, and social dysfunction in the lives of working-class whites took hold as the blue-collar economic heyday of the early 1970s ended and continued through the 2008 financial crisis and the subsequent slow recovery."[27] The growing forms of economic instability that undergird these "deaths of despair" are rooted in the upward redistribution of wealth that began in the early 1970s as well as the dismantling of a broad range of income security programs—attacks on the safety net that occurred over the last thirty years with little objection from white low-income voters or their representatives. As a result, social insurance programs that historically protected low-income white families thrown into crisis by economic transformations and dislocation are no longer available. Here, white workers, believing in their autonomy and self-sufficiency, remained silent while the broad redistributory functions of the state were being dismantled, imagining those cuts would discipline those on the other side of the racial divide. In doing so, they disciplined themselves.

If material conditions alone formed the basis for feelings of hopelessness, African Americans and Latino/as (and Black and Latina women in particular) who contend with much higher rates of discrimination, economic insecurity, and other forms of privation would express the highest feelings of despair. But another recent study finds the exact opposite, explaining that for low-income whites with less formal education "their situation is characterized by lack of hope and aspirations for the future, high levels of unemployment, stark markers of poor health, such as diabetes, obesity, and drug and alcohol addiction, and rising mortality rates driven by preventable deaths from causes such as suicide and opioid poisoning—particularly (but not only) among the middle aged. These trends stand in sharp contrast to high levels of optimism and psychological resilience, gradually improving health indicators, and a closing of the gap in mortality rates among their poor black and Hispanic counterparts."[28]

In this context, how do we make sense of Ruth Wilson Gilmore's influential definition of racism as "the state-sanctioned or extralegal production and exploitation of group-differentiated vulnerability to premature death" when among some groups, whiteness seems to be a marker of *greater* vulnerability to early death?[29] An increase in morbidity and mortality cannot be taken as some sign of a racially egalitarian turn. Instead, we need to reevaluate the assumption that whiteness reliably provides a kind of material and social floor below which those marked as white cannot fall. The racialized safety net and state investments in whiteness have themselves been transformed. As Nikhil Pal Singh and Thuy Linh Tu have observed, "What we are seeing in this moment is not a literal diminishment of white bodies, but the stagnation of these wages of whiteness."[30]

What does this mean, then, in the words of James Baldwin, for "those who think of themselves as white?"[31] In his groundbreaking 1998 study, *The Possessive Investment in Whiteness*, George Lipsitz explained, "Whiteness has a cash value: it accounts for advantages that come to individuals through profits made from housing secured in discriminatory markets, through the unequal educations allocated to children of different races, through insider networks that channel employment opportunities to the relatives and friends of those who have profited most from present and past racial discrimination, and especially through intergenerational transfers of inherited wealth that pass on the spoils of discrimination to succeeding generations." He argues that "white Americans are encouraged to invest in whiteness, to remain true to an identity that provides them with resources, power, and opportunity." For Lipsitz, "investment denotes time spent on a given end" requiring a consideration of the "social and cultural forces [that] encourage white people to expend time and energy on the creation and re-creation of whiteness."[32]

Lipsitz's work demonstrates the ways these dynamics operated across the post–World War II era to structure differential life opportunities and material advantages for hundreds of millions of people. The cumulative effects of these structures are staggering; median white household wealth today is ten times the median wealth of Black households and eight times that of Latino/a households.[33] But if the "cash value" of whiteness appears to be in decline, at least for some segment of those people who think of themselves as white, how might that shape their investments—their use of time to a given end? And how might it change the orientation of particular political formations, among Republicans and (most) Democrats alike, whose political strategy has long sustained the assumption that white racial identity is a proxy for a set of qualities (the virtuous and self-sufficient producer) that provides protection from destitution and indigence?

Racializing White Precarity

For the elites who have abandoned their commitment to the economic protections, institutional supports, and redistribution programs that supported white working- and middle-class people, the growth in white economic precarity raises a daunting problem: How will elites describe and explain the fates of those "virtuous producers" who now find themselves destitute and downwardly mobile?

One response has been a growing tendency to advance cultural and even biological explanations for the expansion of white vulnerability, placing a greater number of whites in discursive categories once reserved for people of color as white poverty is increasingly framed through explanations of dependence, criminality, family disorganization, and genetic deficiency. The anti-Black tropes of cultural and familial degradation proposed by Moynihan's 1965 *The Negro Family* now circulate in explanations of white poverty.

Particularly interesting for our purposes are the ways in which caricatures of genetic degradation found in Richard Herrnstein and Charles Murray's 1994 book, *The Bell Curve*, that explain and naturalize the subordinated status of Black people are now brought to bear on some white subjects. Met with great controversy and criticism when published, *The Bell Curve* argued that a "cognitive elite" emerged in the twentieth century that was disconnected from a much larger population with lower average IQ. Building on a long line of hereditarian thought dating to the nineteenth century that viewed economic and social hierarchies as expressions of cognitive differences, the authors contended that intelligence was a mixture of environmental and genetic inheritance that could be mapped through racial categories. In a chapter titled "Ethnic Differences in Cognitive Ability" they offered a schema that concentrated whites and East Asians in larger proportions at the higher end of the cognitive ability spectrum while African Americans were concentrated at the bottom.[34]

In his 2012 book, *Coming Apart: The State of White America 1960–2010*, Charles Murray continued to argue that a cognitive hierarchy in the United States explains social inequality, but now no longer exempted whites from charges of intellectual inferiority.

He proposed instead what is in effect a new racial category made up of the white poor, constituted by transposing long-standing tropes attached to Blackness (around cognitive capacity and cultural norms) onto destitute whites.

Why has Murray shifted his focus from traditional racial categorizations to elaborate new differentiations among whites? He argues that for decades, sociological research on "trends in American life" has used racial categories with whites as the reference point. "But," he writes, "this strategy has distracted our attention from the way that the reference point itself is changing." Murray argues that the white poor have become behaviorally similar to the Black poor he had described in previous work in terms of declining marriage rates, out-of-wedlock births, aversion to work, and increased criminality; and cognitively similar to them in terms of genetic inheritance. Under the chapter titles "Marriage," "Industriousness," "Honesty," and "Religiosity," Murray portrays a socially disorganized, unmotivated, dependent, morally deficient, and even genetically debased population. Murray's shifting racialization parallels the economic, political, and social changes that have disorganized the assurances many white Americans took for granted during the postwar era. He turns to long-standing racist depictions of Black poverty and culture to narrate and explain the downward mobility of a growing group of impoverished whites, thus indemnifying the role of structural forces in this process. Poverty thus could not be addressed by state interventions or redistributions of wealth, but only by remedying cultural dysfunction and isolation. The billionaire conservative media tycoon Rupert Murdoch captured this implication directly when he tweeted, following the book's release: "Charles Murray's big new study getting great attention. COMING APART. Class divide, not class war. Strongly recommend."[35]

The flagship U.S. conservative weekly *National Review* has similarly pathologized white poverty by transposing long-standing racist tropes to explain the fate of impoverished white communities. In a 2014 article titled "The White Ghetto," Kevin Williamson offered a vivid portrait of Appalachia, employing descriptions of cultural dysfunction that a generation ago were almost exclusively used against people of color. "You have the pills and the dope, the morning beers . . . the federally funded ritual of trading cases of food-stamp Pepsi for packs of Kentucky's Best cigarettes and good old hard currency . . . the occasional blast of meth . . . petty crime, the draw (welfare) . . . recreational making and surgical unmaking of teenaged mothers, and death," writes Williamson. "If the people here weren't 98.5 percent white, we'd call it a reservation."[36]

Again, these descriptions do not supplant or displace enduring accounts of racialized poverty but rather extend them. For Williamson, the term "reservation" stands in for cultural failure and decline, a legible reference in a long and genocidal history of settler-colonial political discourse. Similarly, Williamson uses anti-Black narratives as a touchstone to explain how white poverty and social disorganization have similar roots: "Like its black urban counterparts, the Big White Ghetto suffers from a whole trainload of social problems," he writes, "but the most significant among them may be adverse selection: Those who have the required work skills, the academic ability, or the simple desperate native enterprising grit to do so get the hell out as fast as they can, and they have been doing that for decades."[37]

Following a familiar conservative script, Williamson attributes the crisis in Appalachia to a culture of dependency enabled by the anti-poverty programs of Johnson's Great Society. When Johnson originally proposed an "unconditional war on poverty" as he toured eastern Kentucky, he emphasized that what would become the Great Society was not just meant for urban Black America. It makes sense then that as the white poor become new targets of pathology in conservative arguments for austerity, Appalachia is a tactically useful entry point.

In another *National Review* story two years later, Williamson highlighted not merely cultural pathology but also personal failure and culpability, a narrative long used to justify Black subordination and immiseration. The "white working class," Williamson explained, "failed themselves." He continued, "If you spend time in hardscrabble, white upstate New York, or eastern Kentucky, or my own native West Texas, and you take an honest look at the welfare dependency, the drug and alcohol addiction, the family

NATIONAL REVIEW

The Tragedy
of the Hollows

A REPORT FROM APPALACHIA, WHERE THE COUNTRY IS
BEAUTIFUL AND THE SOCIETY IS BROKEN

Kevin D. Williamson

"The Tragedy of the Hollows," cover for story by Kevin D. Williamson in *National Review*, December 16, 2013.

anarchy . . . you will come to an awful realization. It wasn't Beijing. It wasn't even Washington, as bad as Washington can be. It wasn't immigrants from Mexico, excessive and problematic as our current immigration levels are. It wasn't any of that. Nothing happened to them. There wasn't some awful disaster. There wasn't a war or a famine or a plague or a foreign occupation. Even the economic changes of the past few decades do very little to explain the dysfunction and negligence—and the incomprehensible malice—of poor white America. . . . The white American underclass is in thrall to a vicious, selfish culture whose main products are misery and used heroin needles."[38]

David French, a senior writer at the *National Review*, quickly endorsed Williamson's account, explaining, "Simply put, [white] Americans are killing themselves and destroying their families at an alarming rate. No one is making them do it. The economy isn't putting a bottle in their hand. Immigrants aren't making them cheat on their wives or snort OxyContin. Obama isn't walking them into the lawyer's office to force them to file a bogus disability claim. For generations, conservatives have rightly railed against deterministic progressive notions that put human choices at the mercy of race, class, history, or economics. Those factors can create additional challenges, but they do not relieve any human being of the moral obligation to do their best. Yet millions of Americans aren't doing their best. Indeed, they're barely trying."[39] Expelled from any of these accounts are all the developments over the last fifty years that structured the material condition of so many households: attacks on unions and collective bargaining rights; the stagnation of wages and household income; the ravaging of the social safety net; and the many forms of financial predation and plunder that drive inequality.

J. D. Vance's best-selling memoir, *Hillbilly Elegy: A Memoir of Family and Culture in Crisis*, participates in this same narrative structure of dysfunction and failure, even as it pleads for greater national attention to the latest incarnation of "forgotten Americans." Vance, a self-identified conservative, recounts the range of crises—economic, physical, and emotional—that his family endured in a semirural Ohio town in the midst of industrial decline and economic abandonment. And while his narrative evinces a personal sympathy for the neighbors and kin whom he proudly claims as hillbillies, that descriptor also becomes useful when he seeks to account for their misfortunes. Describing the customers in a local market where he worked as a young adult, he writes: "They'd buy two dozen-packs of soda with food stamps and then sell them at a discount for cash. They'd ring up their orders separately, buying food with food stamps, and beer, wine, and cigarettes with cash. . . . Most of us were struggling to get by, but we made do, worked hard, and hoped for a better life. But a large minority was content to live off the dole. Every two weeks, I'd get a small paycheck and notice the line where federal and state income taxes were deducted from my wages. At least as often, our drug-addict neighbor would buy T-bone steaks, which I was too poor to buy for myself but was forced by Uncle Sam to buy for someone else."[40]

Ultimately, Vance explains that these failures of family, morality, and dependence have produced a culture that "increasingly encourages social decay instead of counteracting it."[41] Elizabeth Catte notes that both the *National Review* and Charles Murray have enthusiastically endorsed *Hillbilly Elegy*.[42] Indeed, Mona Charen argued in the *National Review* that the plight of Vance's family and his hometown should be understood as identical to Murray's *Coming Apart* but "told in the first person." Vance's work demonstrates how "the white working class has followed the black underclass and Native Americans not just into family disintegration, addiction, and other pathologies, but also perhaps into the most important self-sabotage of all, the crippling delusion that they cannot improve their lot by their own effort."[43] The conservative American Enterprise Institute organized a panel with both Vance and Murray titled "The Decline of the White Working Class," explaining that both authors "explore the role of culture, individual circumstance, and responsibility in the social and economic decline of the white working class."[44]

However, it is not just conservatives who have pathologized the white poor. Liberals have also taken up describing impoverished whites in terms once reserved for African Americans. In his 2015 book, *Our Kids: The American Dream in Crisis,* the noted political scientist and author of the popular book *Bowling Alone* Robert Putnam tries to make sense of the yawning economic gap that has produced a significant white lumpenproletariat. Yet instead of focusing on structural explanations, Putnam links economic phenomena to culture and behavior, much as Moynihan did in 1965. "The collapse of the traditional family hit the black community earliest and hardest," he writes, "in part because that community was already clustered at the bottom of the economic hierarchy. That led observers to frame the initial discussion of the phenomenon in racial terms, as Daniel Patrick Moynihan did in his controversial 1965 report, *The Negro Family: The Case for National Action.* But it would turn out that white families were not immune to the changes, and with the benefit of hindsight it's clear that from about 1965 to 1980, American family life underwent a massive transformation."[45]

While Putnam sees economic disparity as a causal factor in the radically reduced prospects for the poor, he, like Murray, makes family central as well. "The collapse of the working-class family," he writes, "is a central contributor to the growing opportunity gap."[46] Thus, just as Moynihan's report sought to explain Black poverty through the lens of moral decay, heteropatriarchal family breakdown, and social deviance, so now do explanations of white poverty from scholars ranging from Murray to Putnam. In foregrounding the cultural and familial traits that make some white workers unfit to succeed in the market, they draw on a long history of racist explanations for inequality that disregarded the forces of economic exploitation and abandonment.

In this sense, the racialization of white poverty can be described as a process of racial transposition, though it is important to be clear about what is being transposed. The subjects of Murray's, Vance's, and Putnam's opprobrium are not occupying the racialized position of Black people or other people of color, nor has the inheritance or ongoing impact of racial subordination been upset. The reorganization of white economic and social privilege in the age of inequality is not totalizing. The legacy of many generations of investment in whiteness as a form of property and value endures and continues to structure life opportunities.[47] The trillions of public and private dollars that white households retain in retirement and investment accounts, social security, home values, and employment and educational opportunities made possible by this long history of white racial preference continues to provide economic security for many white families. Conversely, the disinvestment, abandonment, and asset stripping that prevented the accumulation of wealth in many communities of color makes those households much more economically, politically, and socially vulnerable.

Instead, explanations of dependency, behavioral pathos, family breakdown, and cultural dysfunction that have long been used to contrast Black failure with white success are now summoned and deployed to discipline white workers around privatized market logics. As some of the central conditions in the postwar economic, political, and social settlement have changed, the (economic) wages of whiteness are no longer guaranteed. The legibility of efforts to explain these new forms of privation as effects of cultural degeneracy and dependence is premised upon an enduring racialized logic and domination that has long naturalized white supremacy. They are rooted in a social vision based on categories of worth and unworthiness that ignores structural explanations of inequality and invites scrutiny into the failures or successes of the individual body and family.

Precarious White Rage

As the privileges and securities associated with whiteness are being reorganized, we can expect many white subjects to resist a decline in the social and material status promised on the basis of race and attempt to reverse the declining returns their investments in whiteness have historically afforded them. These transformed conditions shape the ways in which white political identity becomes mobilized, inhabited, contested, and transformed in the context of crisis and abandonment. Race thus continues to perform critical political labor.[48]

Indeed, the 2016 presidential campaign of Donald Trump is an expression of such resistance to changes in the GOP and in the

United States more generally. While these shifts in the racial order are meaningful, two conditions must be stressed: first, like all political shifts, they are partial and incomplete; second, the economic and social changes underfoot have also produced countervailing political movements, efforts that seek to resuscitate the economic, political, and social guarantees of whiteness that characterized much of the postwar period. This white racial revolt was most explicit during Trump's candidacy and election, which linked anxious racial standing to economic precarity and fears of political abandonment. Trump offered a narrative about the debasement of whiteness, recited through accounts of state failure, an anemic military, the loss of national economic standing, and the incursion of racialized foreigners into the U.S. polity.

Trump's first foray into contemporary presidential politics came in 2011, when he challenged the veracity of President Obama's birth certificate and reenergized the "birther" movement's claims that Obama had neither the authority nor the legitimacy to serve as president. For Trump and many other birthers, the claim not only challenged the authority of Obama's legislative and political agenda but also served to index the decline in the sovereignty of the white polity.[49] Obama's victory, and his alleged success in defrauding the U.S. electoral system, revealed the declining autonomy of the virtuous white populace.

Similarly, when Trump announced his candidacy for the Republican nomination in June 2015, he famously insisted that Mexico was "sending people that have lots of problems. . . . They're bringing drugs. They're bringing crime. They're rapists." He framed these comments explicitly through the language of national loss, asking, "When do we beat Mexico at the border? They're laughing at us, at our stupidity." He insisted in his Super Tuesday speech during the Republican primary that "Mexican leaders and negotiators are much tougher and smarter than those of the U.S. Mexico is killing us on jobs and trade. WAKE UP!"[50] To demonstrate the decline of U.S. self-determination, Trump portrays a "Mexico" in the imagination as a place beset by corruption, violence, criminality, and terror that still imposes its will against the United States.

Cheryl Harris argues that historically, whiteness can be conceptualized as analogous to property because of its dependence on the "right to exclude."[51] Here, then, the perceived loss of autonomy over borders, immigration policy, strength in trade deals, or the distribution of foreign aid registers the loss of a central trait of white authority—the power to exclude. Exhortations to "build a wall" on the border with Mexico, which drew wild applause at campaign rallies across the country, can be understood as a reassertion of such authority.[52] Trump's calls for a "Muslim ban" and heightened forms of national and religious government registration and tracking operate similarly.

Indeed, Trump's campaign was also rife with explicit references to permanent loss and failure. While his campaign slogan was "Make America Great Again," Trump constantly foregrounded themes of defeat and abandonment. All along the campaign trail Trump told crowds: "We don't win anymore." "We don't make anything." "We are losing so much." Unlike the leaders of past populist revolts, Trump seemed less a champion of working people than a figure who confirmed their debased status, reveling in such terms as "disgust," "weakness," "losing," and "pathetic."

Thus, Trump's candidacy and his mobilization of white rage can be read as reaction to the declining guarantees that whiteness has provided. This is not to say that Trump was elected by the "white working class"—a long-reified concept that has been revived by both conservatives and progressives to describe Trump voters. These narratives obscure the central role that white middle- and upper-income voters played within Trump's electoral coalition, misrepresent the relationship between economic standing and support for Trump, and conflate race and class status. Yet fears of decline in economic status animated white voters across income levels, fears made meaningful through appeals to racism, nativism, and the power to exclude.

Like the champions of the 2016 Brexit vote in the United Kingdom and the rise of nationalist, anti-immigrant parties and movements in Europe, Trump summons a racial populism to sustain the fantasy that economic inequality and the vulnerability it produces can be avenged through attacks on immigrants and people of color, a fortification of national borders (and more invasive policing within those borders), and an economic nationalism that disavows the dependence of the U.S. economy on the labor of workers and capital from across the globe. It is in many ways a demand for the state to reinvest and to protect the historic value of whiteness, to renew whiteness as a form of "treasured property" premised on the power to exclude. Trumpism itself is only legible as a viable political project through an understanding of the ways that whiteness has long been perceived to provide a basic protection to those racialized as white.

Several prominent opinion polls and focus groups conducted during the election demonstrate the complex links between Trumpism and a sense of the declining value of white racial identity. Notably, these studies report that direct experiences of economic crisis and hardship alone did not necessarily predict support for Trump. One of the largest studies based on Gallup polling data found that Trump supporters "earn relatively high household incomes and are no less likely to be unemployed or exposed to competition through trade or immigration."[53] A poll by the Public Religion Research Institute (PRRI) suggested that "being in fair or poor financial shape actually predicted support for Hillary Clinton among white working-class Americans, rather than support for Donald Trump."[54] The PRRI poll also found that a voter's "gender, age, region and religious affiliation" were not significant predictors of support for Trump, nor were "views about gender roles and attitudes about race."

The measures that did predict support for Trump in the PRRI poll instead seem to capture anxieties about the declining value of whiteness and the protections it would afford. Agreement with statements such as "today discrimination against whites has become as big a problem as discrimination against blacks and other minorities" strongly predicted support for Trump, as did measures about the perceived "foreign influence" on the "American way of life," measures of economic fatalism, and demand for heightened immigration restrictions. While these attitudes have been described as a feeling of being a "stranger in one's own land," that narrative must be placed in a particular context. Trump supporters are actually slightly more likely than other voters to live in racially segregated (white) communities. The feelings of estrangement registered by the study thus do not seem to describe or articulate demographic, social, or cultural transformations within the lived experiences of these respondents.[55] Instead, they capture more abstract perceptions of deterioration, fatalism, and the declining remunerations of whiteness and its protections from vulnerability. The political scientists Justin Gest, Tyler Reny, and Jeremy Mayer have described such perceptions as grounded in "nostalgic deprivation—the discrepancy between individuals' understandings of their current status and their perceptions about their past."[56]

Research by the public-policy scholars Shannon Monnat and David Brown immediately after the 2016 election found that Trump outperformed 2012 Republican nominee Mitt Romney the most in counties with the highest levels of economic distress and "deaths of despair." While Monnat and Brown's study suggests that these relationships are associative rather than causal, the findings intimate a link between the rising mortality rates among white, middle-aged, high-school-educated men and women and support for Trump.[57] We want to highlight the enduring connection between perceptions of fatalism and decline and the embrace of a figure (Trump) and a political movement premised on the regeneration of whiteness and the power to exclude. If we read these developments through the framework of historian Carol Anderson's account of the continued regeneration of "white rage" against perceptions of Black advancement and white decline, we can see them as likely to produce further episodes of crisis, violence, and upheaval.[58]

The Silent Majority Unmoored

On April 10, 2018, in the midst of heightened attention to special counsel Robert Mueller's investigation into the Trump campaign's potential collusion with foreign agents, the Trump–Pence campaign sent a financial solicitation to its supporters. It began, "Let me be clear. Since Day One, this witch hunt has never been about me. *Their target is you.* The swamp doesn't want you to take your country back, and they will fight to the bitter end to stop you."[59]

The solicitation's gesture—what's good for me is good for you—captures clearly the ways political leaders construct interests to bind the identification of supporters to themselves. In this case it also recapitulates and invokes a long-standing language of white cross-class identification, summoned to defend and naturalize white-supremacist political orders as representing the best interests of all those who think of themselves as white. But as Singh and Tu note, "the open secret that Trump's politics conceals is that white privilege no longer provides much protection from economic insecurity." Trump's promise to "return to American greatness through a reinflation of the wages of whiteness" will not address the conditions of what they describe as "morbid capitalism."[60]

Trump's unanticipated rise serves as confirmation that the white producerist order of the twentieth century is no longer dominant in U.S. politics. The political bloc that imagines itself as the Silent Majority has become unmoored, as at least some of its adherents no longer experience the same remunerations of whiteness. Unlike an earlier period, it no longer can constitute an electoral majority in U.S. politics. Republican strategists who have long secured the party's fortunes through appeals to this bloc are rethinking these commitments, witnessed in growing (if still bungled) efforts to appeal to more voters of color. As narrated by Trump, the Silent Majority now invokes an increasingly unstable political identity, one that has at times been unapologetic about the use of violence and intimidation as ordinary practices of politics. As national GOP elites attempt to expand the base of the party by making multicultural appeals while also pursuing economic policies that further widen the gap between the very rich and everyone else, opportunities for the growth of powerfully racist and nativist politics abound. Singh and Tu observe that "terminal whiteness will not be restored to its past glories by reindustrialization, border walls, or the repeated invocation of racial enemies (old or new). That these ideas are now put forth as answers to economic distress merely reflects a deepening of morbid symptoms that have come to define America's racial-capitalist order over the past several decades."[61]

The scholarship and political activism that has foregrounded race as a central dividing line helps us to recognize the many ways that the structural, institutional, and discursive settlements of the postwar era continue to have profound effects on political culture and life possibilities in the United States. The recurrent crisis of racist police and vigilante violence across the nation, the persistent use of racist invective by some political candidates, and the racialized disparities in health, education, housing, and many other realms of social and political life demand an analysis that attends to the historic continuities of racial domination. At the same time, undeniable shifts in material conditions and discursive frameworks require equally careful attention. As the Trump movement has already demonstrated, dangerous forms of white populism will likely develop both inside and outside the party system—although, as we argue in the next two chapters, this authoritarian nationalism based on appeals to a vulnerable whiteness is itself open to unlikely forms of racial transposition.

3

"ONE OF OUR OWN"

Black Incorporations into
Contemporary Conservative Politics

• • •

In 2011 the American Conservative Union announced that Florida congressman Allen West would deliver the coveted closing keynote address at the annual Conservative Political Action Conference (CPAC). A few months earlier, West became the first African American Republican elected to represent the state since the end of Reconstruction; his election was backed by an outpouring of right-wing grassroots support. David Keene, CPAC organizer and chair of the American Conservative Union, declared that Congressman West was "one of our own" who "epitomizes the core conservative values CPAC attendees treasure: a basic belief in human freedom, traditional values, and a love of country based on an appreciation of the nation's founding documents."[1]

West caught the attention of conservatives nationally after delivering a fiery address to a 2009 Tea Party rally in Fort Lauderdale, telling the audience, "We have a class warfare that's going on. You've got a producing class, and you've got an entitlement class." West narrated his own story, rising from "the inner city of Atlanta" to serving for twenty-two years in the military and "leading men and women into combat," as a tale not just of racial striving but of U.S. exceptionalism rooted in market freedoms, military might, and a deep antipathy toward the state. He never suggested this "entitlement class" was Black or brown or relegated to the inner city. "These people," he explained, "are living in and amongst us" and were poised, like the wayward public-sector workers discussed in chapter 1, to bring the nation to its knees. West concluded to the Tea Party faithful, "If you are ready to stand up, to get your musket, to fix your bayonet and to charge into the ranks, then you are my brother or sister in this fight."[2] The overwhelmingly white audience gave West a wild ovation, and a video of the speech soon went viral in conservative circles, garnering millions of views on YouTube.[3]

West's address to nearly eleven thousand CPAC attendees did not disappoint. He celebrated the free market, tax cuts, the private sector, and limited government, warning that "we cannot continue with a public sector that is out-taking the private sector" and that the nation could not "survive as a bureaucratic nanny state." He made plain his hostility to reproductive rights and venerated the patriarchal family. He reiterated his long-standing commitment to a robust militarism, explaining that while serving in Iraq in the early 2000s he "stood on the wall to tell his country, 'sleep peacefully at night because this man stands ready to do the violence and things necessary to protect you.'" Elements of his extreme rhetoric anticipated the violent ultra-nationalism that would mark the Trump campaign five years hence, such as his unapologetic critique of "radical Islamist belligerents who transport the seventh century ideologies that are anathema to the values of American and Western Civilization."

And as in his Tea Party rally address, West narrated his conservative commitments through his personal life and trajectory, with explicit references to his roots as a working-class Black southerner. He explained that his parents, who were "nicknamed Buck and Snooks," sent him to school "across the street from the Baptist Church" and that as a child growing up in rural Randolph County, Georgia, he climbed pecan trees and was "brought up to say 'pea-can.'"

Stories of Black folkish authenticity pitched at white audiences are hardly new; Clarence Thomas continually framed his life story in these terms during his confirmation to the U.S. Supreme Court in 1991.[4] But what makes West's invocation of these tropes at CPAC and elsewhere distinct is that he offered them as exemplars not of a particularistic Black tradition but as exemplars of conservatism writ large, the purest significations of the enduring value of militarism, patriotism, and an ethic of striving and self-sufficiency. He described at length the scorn he faced from the media and the liberal establishment for being a Black conservative, explicitly connecting his experiences to the condescension and derision that those in the audience continually faced from the same forces. His bravery, in the face of this smug hostility and derision, was for them. He concluded his speech, "This son of America stands before you on this grand stage committing himself to his country, to its national character, to its fiscal and national security, to the preservation of the life, liberty, and pursuit of happiness of every American. . . . I do it for the men and women in uniform. I do it for the little boy and little girl wearing a high school junior ROTC uniform just like I did. I do it for the unborn American child."[5] The crowd erupted in deafening applause and a standing ovation. "One of our own" indeed.

While West's single term in Congress was marked by controversy—he insisted in a town hall meeting that at least seventy-eight Democrats in Congress were members of the Communist Party—his ascension within the contemporary GOP is far from aberrant.[6] West is among an important cohort of Black conservatives who have stepped onto the national stage since the Tea Party's emergence in 2009, including Senator Tim Scott of South Carolina, Representative Mia Love of Utah, 2012 presidential candidate Herman Cain, and 2016 presidential candidate and Housing and Urban Development (HUD) secretary Dr. Ben Carson.[7] Indeed, thirty-two Black Republicans ran for congressional seats in 2012.[8] Other people of color have also become some of the most popular figures among the party's conservative rank and file in recent elections: Louisiana gover-nor Bobby Jindal, South Carolina governor Nikki Haley, Idaho congressman Raul Labrador, Senators Marco Rubio of Florida and Ted Cruz of Texas, and Governors Susana Martinez of New Mexico and Brian Sandoval of Nevada.

These figures, to be sure, vary greatly in their ideological orientation, their emergence within the GOP, and their relationship to contemporary conservatism. In addition, race does different kinds of work in each of these accounts. The immigrant-uplift stories attached to Asian American politicians like Jindal and Haley differ in important ways from the militaristic nationalism of Allen West and the forms of maternal law-and-order politics advanced by a figure like Susana Martinez. But taken together, they suggest subtle transformations in the racialization of electoral politics in general and conservative formations in particular. Of course, organic traditions of Black conservatism stretch back to the late nineteenth century. As scholars including Corey Fields, Joshua Farrington, Timothy Thurber, and Leah Wright Rigueur have demonstrated, while Black conservatives have had an enduring if uneven relationship with the GOP, many continue to find conservative policies and ideals to be commensurate with the self-interests of Black communities.[9] That is, they understand the principles of free markets and limited government, and more recently restrictions on immigration and reproductive rights, as facilitating Black uplift and Black social, political, and economic power. Angela Dillard argued in the early 2000s that "American political conservatism can no longer be viewed, and accurately represented, as the exclusive preserve of white, male, and heterosexual persons with comfortable class positions."[10]

The figures we examine in this chapter, however, differ in important ways from previous generations of conservatives of color in general and Black conservatives in particular. This is not because their emergence can be read (as many conservative partisans would have it) as a kind of triumphalist color-blind ideology that has overtaken an earlier history of racial exclusion and subordination. The base and profile of the contemporary Republican Party is as white, conservative, and Christian as it has ever been, and its policy positions and budget priorities only strengthen long-standing racial hierarchies. In many areas of the South in particular, the GOP is effectively an all-white party.[11] The emergence of these figures also does not represent a realignment in the racialized patterns of partisanship that have crystallized nationally in the last thirty years. Since 1964, at least 80 percent of Black voters have cast their ballot for the Democratic nominee for president.[12] Obama secured 95 percent of the Black vote in 2008 and 93 percent in 2012. The *Washington Post* reported that the 2016

Republican National Convention (RNC) had the fewest number of Black delegates for any such meeting in the last one hundred years (both as a percentage and as an absolute number)—only 18 out of 2,472 delegates total.[13] In the 2016 presidential election, Donald Trump garnered only 6 percent of the Black vote and less than 20 percent of the Latino/a vote, though men in both groups voted for Trump at significantly higher rates than did women in those groups.[14]

Given these dynamics and the GOP's record of antipathy during the last fifty years toward any remediation of racial hierarchy and inequality, why do subjects like West, Scott, and Love come to serve as exemplars of contemporary white conservatism—indeed, among its most celebrated figures? How does their racial identity serve to legitimate commitments to market freedoms, anti-statism, militarized authority, and exclusionary immigration politics?

What makes these figures different, we argue, is that their racialized subjectivities do not simply function to discipline or scold other Black people and people of color from embracing anti-racist or redistributory politics. Since 1965 the dominant mode of Black incorporation within conservatism—witnessed in figures including Thomas Sowell, Shelby Steele, Ward Connerly, and Clarence Thomas and in journals like *Destiny* and *Lincoln Review*—has focused on the alleged failures of affirmative action programs and critiques of the state as they relate to race. These conservatives of color (we could also include here figures like the writer Dinesh D'Souza) were primarily authorized to address matters of race from a conservative perspective and to critique those demanding more robust state intervention into discrimination. Their role and imperative was clear: to discredit left/liberal critiques of state-sponsored anti-discrimination measures and those who would demand greater state intervention into racial and social equality.[15]

By contrast, race functions differently for West, Scott, and Love, particularly in relation to their base of white conservative voters. At a time of growing precarity and vulnerability for many white households, we argue that they become the idealized subjects of the marketized and militarized nation, continually testifying to its exceptional qualities at a time of crisis. For West, Scott, and Love, race not only stands in as an ethical and redemptive subjectivity that works to reinforce and naturalize a host of ideas central to modern conservatism; it also symbolizes a kind of outsider status with which many white conservatives have come to identify.

From this perspective, the rise in the number of people of color within the GOP is not simply a tactical measure or an instrumental maneuver to expand the party's electoral share among voters of color. Nor is it only window dressing intended to disavow and distract from the party's long-standing hostility toward racial justice. West, Love, and Scott all defeated white conservative opponents to win election in districts dominated by white conservative voters. These figures instead exemplify more profound changes in the ways race is being deployed within dominant modes of neoliberal governance and electoral politics and in the shaping of popular consent under conditions of growing precarity and crisis. As we explain, these developments, nurtured by Democrats and Republicans alike, can be traced to the uneven trajectory and incorporation of Black social movements since the early 1970s, in which symbols of Blackness have become increasingly unmoored from their radical and oppositional legacies.[16]

"Think Your Way Out of Poverty": The Rise of Senator Tim Scott

The First Congressional District in South Carolina hugs the southern coast of the Palmetto state, including the tidal and barrier sea islands of Charleston, Colleton, and Beaufort Counties. Historically, it has extended from the Santee River south to the Georgia border, incorporating much of the city of Charleston.[17] During Reconstruction, newly enfranchised Black voters in the district elected to four consecutive terms freedman Joseph H. Rainey, the first African American to serve in the House.[18]

The Republican Party's relationship to racial politics in the South has a complex history. The party emerged in the 1850s as a distinctly antislavery formation. Its candidate barely won a four-way contest in the presidential election of 1860, but afterward it prosecuted the Civil War, became the party of Black emancipation, and then became the party of Reconstruction. Rainey championed many of the landmark civil rights laws of the Reconstruction period before losing his seat in 1878 to a Confederate Civil War veteran. Reactionary forces in the South and North aligned to defeat the project of Reconstruction, and by 1877 the party slowly abandoned its commitment to full Black citizenship.

By 1896, with Black voters effectively disenfranchised across the state, the district elected a series of white Democratic representatives, whose hostility to civil rights and anti-discrimination politics was unbroken. In the 1930s Black loyalty to the Republican Party eroded quickly in favor of the Democratic New Deal.[19] It was not that Franklin Delano Roosevelt and the national party offered anything distinct in the way of a substantive Black political program, such as the promotion of anti-lynching legislation or an end to Jim Crow rule in the South. But facing forms of economic exploitation and poverty, African Americans had much more to gain economically from the Democrats than the Republicans. Roosevelt won 71 percent of the Black vote in 1936.[20]

From the 1960s through the 1980s the modern Republican Party reinvented itself by mobilizing and extending a critique of state power as a way of constructing white opposition to Black freedom. The GOP during this time—a span Joseph Lowndes has described as the "Goldwater to Atwater" period—built its electoral fortunes *against* Blackness by making appeals (both explicit and coded) to white racial identity and interests. The racialized markers of the modern Republican Party—the Southern Strategy, the Silent Majority, Nixon's demands for "law and order," Reagan's "welfare queens," and George H. W. Bush's "Willie Horton" campaign—all turned on constructing figures of Black failure and threat to mobilize a cross-class alliance of white voters. Following the lead of prominent segregationist politicians like South Carolina senator Strom Thurmond, white voters in the former Confederate states, who had voted Democratic since the end of the Civil War, began shifting party allegiance to the GOP in the late 1960s.

The first Republican to represent South Carolina's First District since Reconstruction was elected in 1981. From 1987 to 1995 the people's choice was Republican Arthur Ravenel Jr., a proud member of the Sons of Confederate Veterans. At a 2000 rally to defend the raising of the Confederate flag at the state capitol, Ravenel referred to the NAACP as the "National Association for Retarded People."[21] The district's electorate in 2010 was more than 75 percent white, with a large concentration of conservative-leaning voters almost guaranteed to elect a representative from the GOP.

When the seat became vacant in 2010 (and the district redrawn to include the northern section of the coast), two prominent Republicans attached to towering figures within the state's political history emerged as the leading contenders: former prosecutor and Charleston County Council member Paul Thurmond, son of the late Strom Thurmond; and Carroll Campbell III, the son of former governor Carroll Campbell II, a long-standing client of the Republican strategist Lee Atwater, the notorious architect of the 1988 "Willie Horton" presidential campaign advertisements for George H. W. Bush.[22] Both Thurmond and Campbell identified with the nascent Tea Party and promised to undo the Affordable Care Act, reduce taxes, shrink the federal government, and generally oppose the Obama administration at every turn. With the district still dominated by white Republican voters in a solidly conservative state, Campbell or Thurmond seemed assured of winning the seat.[23]

The district's voters, however, overwhelmingly rejected Campbell and Thurmond in favor of businessman Tim Scott, making him the state's first African American Republican elected to Congress since George W. Murray left office in 1897. Scott finished first in the nine-candidate Republican primary before trouncing Thurmond in the runoff, winning a majority in every county in the district.[24] Scott's electoral support only continued to grow. Two years later Governor Nikki Haley appointed Scott to fill the U.S. Senate seat vacated by Jim DeMint, who resigned to assume the presidency of the conservative Heritage Foundation. Scott was at the time the only African American in the Senate. Two years later he defeated numerous white challengers in the Republican Primary and cruised to an easy reelection, and in 2014 he won the largest share of the vote of any statewide candidate running in a two-party contested race.[25] In both the primary and general elections, Scott's support has been strongest in white rural counties and among the state's most conservative voters; his electoral base in this sense is nearly identical to that of President Trump.[26]

Scott's conservative credentials are indeed unimpeachable. A devout evangelical Christian, in the mid-1990s as a member of the Charleston County Council he helped lead an effort to post the Ten Commandments outside the council chambers, personally hanging the document to ensure the body and all speakers adhered to its moral absolutes.[27] In 1996 he had served as honorary co-chairman of Strom Thurmond's final Senate campaign.[28]

Elected to the South Carolina General Assembly in 2008, Scott was staunchly anti-union, introducing a bill to make the state's right-to-work status a cornerstone of its business recruitment strategy. He became an instant favorite among Tea Party and anti-tax groups.[29] In the 2010 Republican primary, Scott won the endorsement of conservative opinion leaders nationally, including former Arkansas governor Mike Huckabee, DeMint, and Sarah Palin, who described him as a "pro-life, pro-2nd Amendment, pro-development, Commonsense Conservative."[30] As a member of Congress, he supported calls to impeach President Obama and proposed a bill to make entire families ineligible for food stamps if one member participated in a labor strike.[31]

In the 2014 election, in which both Scott and incumbent Republican senator Lindsey Graham were up for reelection, a study concluded that while the two senators' bases of electoral support were nearly identical, "one of the few differences was that Tea Party backers and racial conservatives were significantly more supportive of Scott."[32] Indeed, a simple experiment conducted within a South Carolina poll in 2014 found that when Scott was presented to voters through a frame of race (e.g., as "United States Senator Tim Scott, the first African American Senator from South Carolina since Reconstruction") it increased the likelihood among all voters, including self-identified white conservatives, of viewing him more positively compared to when he was introduced through a Tea Party frame (i.e., as "United States Senator and Tea Party favorite Tim Scott").[33] The results suggest that Scott's Blackness made him more appealing to white conservative voters.

A 2015 study based on surveys conducted in 2006, 2010, and 2012 that examined conservative support for Republican candidates of color for governor and the U.S. Senate found that "white conservatives are either more supportive of minority Republicans or just as likely to vote for a minority as they are a white Republican."[34] To be clear, neither study identified or suggested an attenuation in broader racialized attitudes or policy preferences among such conservative voters. That is, they are no less likely to be skeptical of claims about widespread racial discrimination and bias or supportive of affirmative action programs. Yet the same voters hostile to civil rights and anti-discrimination policies energetically support an African American as their standard-bearer. The study's authors concluded that a growing number of conservatives of color should be able to "win Republican primaries and have a strong chance of winning the general-election contest, if the political setting is favorable (e.g., a red state)."[35]

In Scott's case, his success in the general election did not depend on Black voters. An exit poll found that African American support for Scott in 2014 was only 15 percent, the lowest level of any group identified in the survey.[36] Scott has consistently earned an F on the NAACP's annual legislative scorecard, and he even voted to delay funding of a legal settlement in favor of Black farmers who had suffered years of discrimination in lending by the U.S. Department of Agriculture.[37]

After his election to Congress in 2010, Scott announced he would not be joining the Congressional Black Caucus as his "campaign was not about race," rehearsing one of the core shibboleths of color-blind conservatism.[38] He explained that the "relevance of me being black is really, fortunately, irrelevant."[39] He suggested in another interview that at the dozens of Tea Party rallies he has attended and addressed he had yet to encounter a "racist comment" or a "person who approaches me from a racist perspective." Instead, he contended, "the basis of the Tea Party has nothing to do with race. It has to do with an economic recovery. It has to do with limiting the role of our government in our lives. It has to do with free markets."[40] This is a message eagerly repeated by his supporters, who understand their embrace of Scott

Tim Scott speaking at the 2013 South Carolina Tea Party Coalition Convention. From WPDE ABC 15, January 13, 2013.

as evidence of their color-blind commitments, as well as some commentators, who suggest that Scott's election reveals that "ideology trumps race" for white southern conservatives.[41]

In late 2017, Scott stood next to President Trump and House Speaker Paul Ryan during the signing ceremony for the GOP's tax plan—a significant cut to the tax liabilities facing the nation's wealthiest households and corporations. As the ceremony began, a *Huffington Post* blogger named Andy Ostroy tweeted, "What a shocker . . . there's ONE black person there and sure enough they have him standing right next to the mic like a manipulated prop. Way to go @SenatorTimScott." Scott here was charged with being a token offered to give the GOP's overwhelmingly white and male leadership some nominal cover. But Scott's reply to Ostroy on Twitter after the press conference offered a different account: "Uh probably because I helped write the bill for the past year, have multiple provisions included, got multiple Senators on board over the last week and have worked on tax reform my entire time in Congress. But if you'd rather just see my skin color, pls feel free."[42]

Ostroy's reaction to Scott's presence on the podium spoke to the dominant expectation (at least among liberals) of the role race might play within contemporary conservatism—that is, as prop or distraction. Yet while Ostroy's accusation was erroneous (Scott had indeed worked behind the scenes for months on the legislation), the notion that race plays no role in Scott's public life is equally flawed.

Across his career it is important to note the ways in which Scott's racial identity has remained central to the narratives fashioned to voters in general and his white supporters in particular. The story lines used to introduce him to voters and audiences have linked his Blackness to his conservative commitments in particular ways. Scott makes visible rather than obscures his Black racial identity. In a speech to the 2013 South Carolina Tea Party Convention, Scott opened his comments by mimicking a deep baritone call associated with a Black preacher, declaring, "It's Sunday morning, hah!" He told the crowd he "grew up wanting to be a preacher, but God made me a politician."[43] Scott's comments to conservative audiences, like West's, are riddled with Black southern vernacular. During his 2013 address to CPAC, Scott said that as a teenager he shared a car with his mother because "we were po'. Not poor, p-o-o-r, but p-o. Just po'."[44]

And also like West, Scott chronicles his embrace of conservative ideals as an extension of his childhood experiences. He told CPAC: "I think back to my young days, growing up in a single parent household, I think about the tough times that my mother, who worked 16-hour days—she went to work all day long—came home and when my grades were bad, she would just, pull out the switch. Because my mama loved me a lot, and sometimes she believed that love comes at the end of a switch. And she proved it to me."[45]

As a teenager Scott struggled in high school, nearly dropping out, until he had the "blessing of meeting a conservative Republican who became my mentor. A guy named John Moniz. He was a Chick-Fil-A operator. And John started teaching me some of the most valuable lessons I ever learned. He taught me that having a job is a good thing, but creating jobs is a far better thing. If you have an income, that's a good thing, but if you create a profit, you can do the most amazing things. . . . That was part of my path to becoming a red-blooded conservative. Because he taught me, *how to think my way out of poverty*. And my mother taught me discipline and that combination made such a huge impact on where I am today."[46]

These anecdotes about growing up in a single-parent household, about the lessons from his mother's switch, and receiving guidance as a wayward teenager from a conservative mentor to "think his way out of poverty" have been the bread and butter of Scott's stump speeches. The themes of individual uplift through an unswerving work ethic, self-discipline grounded in familial (and maternal) bonds, and an unrestrained belief in the market's ability to turn paupers into princes are hallmarks of Scott's political narrative. In many ways they are grounded in a long history of Black political ideals, extending from the early days of Reconstruction to much of the recent discourse from the Obama White House. As Lester Spence has demonstrated, these narratives have played an outsize role more recently in some Black evangelical formations, connecting a "prosperity gospel" to a broader political orientation that internalizes neoliberal logics and aspirations and explains conditions such as poverty and debt as the consequences of a "mindset."[47]

But there is an important distinction and transformation to note when these themes are sounded by Scott. Self-help narratives within Black political thought have almost exclusively been addressed to Black publics, often as an answer to crises of poverty, struggle, and vulnerability. They are *Black* self-help politics. The call to "do for yourself" rather than waiting for society and government to ameliorate your pain, as sounded by Booker T. Washington, Black conservatives like Clarence Thomas and Shelby Steele, cultural figures like Bill Cosby, and liberal centrists like Barack Obama and Cory Booker, have been meant to address the alleged flaws and pathologies of Black life, culture, and values.[48]

Scott, by contrast, mobilizes these ideals to a base of supporters that is overwhelmingly white. His story is for them; his experiences are of a piece with theirs. His example is not meant to inspire or shame African Americans. He does not generally talk about issues like welfare, crime, and family formation in racialized terms. And though Scott's policy commitments are antithetical to the material interests of the large majority of African Americans, his rise does not generally follow the well-known pattern of "modern-day Republicans [that] have deployed blacks to undermine black interests."[49] That is not his immediate imperative.

When Scott does talk about his relationship to Black communities, he strikes a different tone. During a 2012 Associated Press interview, he argued that conservatives had to emphasize the benefits and opportunities of capitalism to "people who come from neighborhoods like I came from and simply sell them on the fact that this country is a place where you can rise to any level."[50] He told a reporter after his 2010 election that while he was reluctant to be the "race man" of the GOP, if he were asked to carry a message to Black Democratic voters it would be "Faith in God. . . . School choice and vouchers. And private enterprise. I want people to know that the American Dream is still alive and well, and I'm living proof."[51] He told a *Politico* reporter that "God made me black on purpose. For a specific reason. It has helped me to help others who have been locked out of opportunity in many ways."[52]

Indeed, in other contexts, including three interrelated speeches he gave on the Senate floor in the wake of the police killings of Philando Castile in Minneapolis and Walter Scott in South Carolina in 2015, Scott spoke passionately about the humiliations of racial profiling and stereotyping. He faced no visible backlash from his base of white conservative supporters.[53] The same year, after white supremacist Dylann Roof murdered nine parishioners at Emanuel African Methodist Episcopal Church in Charleston, South Carolina, including state senator Clementa Pinckney, a senior pastor at the church, Scott wept as he read the names of the victims on the Senate floor.[54]

To the extent that Scott's electoral base largely mirrors that of the most conservative members of the GOP, we can reasonably conclude that the same political commitments and values of Trump voters, as established across numerous survey-based data sets described in chapter 2, also apply to backers of Scott: support for restrictionist immigration policies, an antipathy toward increases in racial and ethnic diversity and cultural pluralism, and a perception that whiteness itself has become an object of discrimination, disadvantage, and social stigma.[55] Yet these same voters have elevated Scott to the most influential legislative body in the nation, where he enjoys strong favorability ratings from South Carolina voters in general and his conservative base in particular.[56]

Of Patriots and Pioneers: Mia Love's America

On August 28, 2012, as the remnants of Hurricane Isaac swirled through downtown Tampa Bay, the thirty-seven-year-old mayor of Saratoga Springs, Utah, took to the stage at the Tampa Bay Times Forum at the Republican National Convention. The four-minute speaking slot afforded to Mia Love, scheduled in the midst of more than fifty speakers at the opening day of the convention, was hardly esteemed. The convention hall was restless and noisy as a video introducing Love to the audience began. Looking directly in the camera, Love recalled a conversation with her father as he was dropping her off for her first day at college. "He looked at me very seriously and he said 'Mia, your mother and I have done everything to get you where you are right now. We've never taken a handout. We have worked hard for everything we have had through personal responsibility. You will not be a burden to society. You will give back.'" After the video introduces her as a mother of three young children, a public official, and committed spouse, she continues: "If I could describe freedom in one word, it would be agency. The ability to make decisions. The ability to reap the benefits of those decisions, or suffer the consequences. . . . What makes America great, is that we are free. Free to work, free to live. Free to choose. And free to fail."[57]

Love's parents emigrated from Haiti in 1973 during the maelstrom of political upheaval that followed the death of François "Papa Doc" Duvalier. Love was born in Brooklyn two years later. After graduating from college she converted to Mormonism and moved to Salt Lake City to be closer to the Church of Jesus Christ of Latter-day Saints (LDS). She eventually married Jason Love, a white LDS member, and in 2003 won her first office, a city council seat in Saratoga Springs, a small suburb of about twenty thousand people on the outskirts of Salt Lake City. In 2012 she defeated two white state representatives, Stephen Sandstrom and Carl Wimmer, to win the Republican nomination for the newly created Fourth Congressional District. The district, covering some of Salt Lake City and its suburbs, is nearly 85 percent white and less than 2 percent Black.[58]

As the video ended and Love took the stage at the RNC, the crowd grew quiet. Love's speech made no mention of welfare dependency or attacks on affirmative action; there was no finger-wagging at the inner city. Instead, her experience as a Black immigrant was celebrated as exemplifying the ideals of individual uplift and American exceptionalism. "My parents immigrated to the U.S. with ten dollars in their pocket, believing that the America they had heard about really did exist. When times got tough, they didn't look to Washington, they looked within," Love told the audience. "So the America I came to know was centered in personal responsibility and filled with the American dream." Here again, Love's Blackness is deployed as commensurate with, rather than a negation of, the producerist ethic. "The America I know is grounded in the determination found in patriots and pioneers, in small business owners with big ideas, in the farmers who work in the beauty of our landscape, in our heroic military and Olympians. It's in every child who looks at the seemingly impossible and says, 'I can do that.' That is the America I know!"[59]

The convention hall erupted in applause. Love's campaign reportedly raised some $100,000 in donations in the twenty-four hours following the speech.[60] Love narrowly lost the 2012 election to Democratic congressman Jim Matheson, but she regrouped in 2014 to win both the Republican primary in a landslide, capturing 78 percent of the vote, and the general election, taking a seat from the Democrats and becoming the first Haitian American as well as the first African American Republican woman to serve in Congress. (She was reelected by a comfortable margin in 2016.) Like Scott, Love described her campaign and election as a color-blind triumph, telling CNN shortly after the 2014 election that "this has nothing to do with race. Understand that Utahans have made a statement that they are not interested in dividing Americans based on race or gender. . . . Race and gender had nothing to do with it. Principles had everything to do with it."[61]

Love's biography and narrative differ in important ways from those of Scott and West. Her membership in the LDS, a church that had significant restrictions on Black leadership and membership until 1978, plays an important role in her public identity. And in her stump speech she ties her immigrant roots to her deep identification with the nation and its Horatio Alger mythology wedded to an articulation of "compassionate conservatism" that stresses a privatized mutuality and personal generosity. At a 2015 address to CPAC she explained, "My challenge to the conservative movement is for us to be the group that promotes the ideas and the opportunities where people can come to this country legally like my parents did with ten dollars in their pocket and live their version of the American dream."[62]

She continually recites her father's belief in the nation's promise—and his status as a legally authorized migrant—to narrate her faith in the market and the just role it plays in rewarding winners and punishing losers.[63] If West regularly sounds notes appealing to military might and a masculinized nationalism, Love offers a conservatism that stresses upward mobility and altruism: "We've lifted ourselves up. And made sure that we gave opportunity to anyone that was in need. Given the opportunity we helped the neighbor, we helped the struggling student, parent or friend." This was not an Ayn Rand–animated testimony to the virtues of selfishness, but a story of family uplift and communalism. "We must advance the conservative principles that have lifted more people out of poverty, fueled more freedom and driven more dreams than any set of principles in the history of the world. . . . Imagine a single mother who is trapped in poverty by big government programs that prevent her from taking opportunities and proving that she can rise to the occasion. I believe that that mother can, and will rise—if she is given the opportunity to do so."[64]

While Love did not attend the 2016 RNC, choosing to campaign in her district rather than be present for Trump's nomination, her conservative bona fides are unimpeachable. She has the enthusiastic backing of most Tea Party groups and has spoken openly about dismantling the Department of Education, the Department of Energy, and most income-support programs. Endorsed by the National Rifle Association, she is an ardent defender of gun rights and holds a permit to carry a concealed weapon. She has addressed the March for Life and is a firm opponent of abortion rights and same-sex marriage. She backs the return of public lands in Utah from the federal government to state and local control, a cause dear to militia and patriot groups.[65]

In 2018, a far-right group that had supported Roy Moore's failed candidacy for the Senate in Alabama attempted to raise money to encourage Love to run for the Utah Senate seat vacated by Orrin Hatch, in order to keep the seat away from Mitt Romney.[66]

There are a number of paradoxes to note here. On the one hand, for the period from Goldwater to Atwater it is nearly impossible to imagine an ultra-conservative group mobilizing to elect a Black woman in order to oust a white conservative figure like Romney. By Reagan's election in 1980, race had fully hardened as

Republican congressional candidate Mia Love addresses gun-rights rally and march at the state capitol in Salt Lake City, Utah, March 2, 2013. Photograph by George Frey/Getty Images.

a key electoral factor dividing Republicans from Democrats. Reagan ran against "welfare queens" and for "states' rights"—a racial strategy that won him white votes across regions and socioeconomic statuses. Black politicians, cultural representations of Blackness, and Black uplift stories could not easily stand in for the embattled white producerist bloc, the Silent Majority, or the "forgotten man" during this period. Blackness, at a symbolic level, stood in opposition to those values, constituted by dependence, indolence, and excess. Yet today, figures like Love, West, and Scott can assume commanding positions in the white conservative imaginary. What historical developments and conditions made these forms of incorporation possible?

The Protean Character of Blackness in the Post–Civil Rights Era

The conditions favorable to the emergence of contemporary Black conservatives like West, Love, and Scott have been many decades in the making. In a 1979 article titled "Black Particularity Reconsidered" in the journal *Telos,* the political scientist Adolph Reed describes a series of transitions in the 1970s that helped create such conditions of possibility. In Reed's account, between the mid-1950s and the early 1970s there was "almost constant political motion among blacks" that was both mass-based, rooted in demands for redistribution, and oppositional to many forms of elite authority.[67] We can think here of the rich histories of Black trade unionism, Black internationalism, Black women's grassroots organizing, and the collective mobilizations and self-organization among students, consumers, voters, prisoners, and others that constituted such mass action. This tradition was focused on a broad redistribution of resources, rights, and power rooted in democratic participation.

Reed argues that beginning in the early 1970s, as the first wave of Black leaders and managers became nominally integrated into systems of governance and power, racialized antagonisms became increasingly depoliticized. They shifted toward contests over elite administrative authority rather than a fundamental restructuring of power or resources or a broadened sense of popular democracy.

Reed points to a convergence between the administrative and ideological needs of late-twentieth-century consumer-oriented capitalism and its bureaucratic rationalities and the elite brokerage models of Black political participation and leadership, within both its civil rights and Black Power articulations. This "new mode of administered domination" necessitated the incorporation of Blackness within an increasingly bureaucratized and repressive society that Herbert Marcuse had described in 1964 in his one-dimensionality thesis. Here, forms of elite brokerage politics, exemplified in the rise of hundreds of Black elected officials and administrators, tended "to capitulate to the predominant logic of domination" and were commensurate with the intensification of consumption. Within an increasingly "homogenized American life," symbolic forms of Black incorporation lent prevailing modes of administrative domination an ethical legitimacy and pluralistic connotation. Business and state elites did not directly compel or force these new forms of incorporation; they were the effects of mass-based mobilizations and demands. At the same time, Reed argues, this new Black managerial stratum "stabilized and coordinated the adjustment of the black population to social policy imperatives formulated outside the black community."[68]

We can see these efforts to incorporate narratives of Black uplift within prevailing structures of power within Nixon's presidential campaigns of 1968 and 1972 and in his administration more broadly. At the same time he was addressing the Silent Majority and summoning the specter of Black lawlessness, Nixon recruited a number of Black politicos to his campaign and later gave them presidential appointments.[69] These included Massachusetts senator Edward Brooke, Michigan GOP vice chair Earl Kennedy, Black Power Conference secretary Nathan Wright, Republican Minorities Group leader Clarence Townes, and civil rights advocate Arthur Fletcher. The jazz singer Ethel Ennis sang the National Anthem at Nixon's 1972 reinauguration (drawing a poetic rebuke from June Jordan); the ceremony also included Lionel Hampton and Jackie Robinson. Nixon hoped to win over Black voters on issues of education, safe neighborhoods, and entrepreneurship. He explicitly wedded the notion of Black Power to Black capitalism, and on the campaign trail he spoke about African Americans wanting "a piece of the action."[70] The campaign took out a series of advertisements in *Jet* magazine that suggested an intimacy with Black culture. As political communications scholar Carole Bell wrote regarding the photographs in the ads, "There is also something familiar about the visual language of the portraits as well—perhaps reminiscent of the great African-American photographer Gordon Parks' work."[71]

It was through developments like these, Reed suggests, that the Nixon "blackonomics" strategy was readily able to co-opt and neutralize much of the rebellious tendency of 1960s Black activism. Black "liberation" quickly turned into Black "equity," and the "black elite broadened its administrative control by uncritically assuming the legitimacy of the social context within which that elite operated. Black control was by no means equivalent to democratization."[72] Under these conditions, and "having internalized the predominant elite-pluralist model of organization of black life," Black politics increasingly lost both its mass-based character and its capacity to develop critical perspectives about the modes of domination within which it had been integrated.

THIS TIME VOTE LIKE HENRY GIBBS' WHOLE WORLD DEPENDED ON IT.

Richard Nixon understands the importance of education for the black child. He knows that better schools are the key to a better life. He believes in more federal aid to education to help build better schools in the cities. Mr. Nixon also wants more black teachers and black administrators to give, as Floyd McKissick has said, "A black authority figure with whom our children can identify and to whom they can aspire." The future of children like Henry Gibbs has always depended upon you.

THIS TIME...
NIXON

This One
RLGD-BDS-HSLB

AUTHORIZED AND PAID FOR

Richard Nixon campaign ad in *Jet,* October 17, 1968.

Reed contends that "internal critique could not go beyond banal symbols of 'blackness,'" as "Black Power itself construed racial politics within the ideological universe through which the containment of the black population was mediated."[73] These "banal symbols" stood in for and displaced long traditions of oppositional politics rooted within Black publics. Increasingly, Blackness represented a kind of "otherness" that bureaucratic capitalism needed to demonstrate was not one-dimensional, unitary, and rigid but dynamic, polyglot, soulful, and lively. As Cedric Johnson similarly notes, "insurgent demands for black indigenous control converged with liberal reform initiatives to produce a moderate black political regime and incorporate radical dissent into conventional political channels."[74]

Today, the obsession with certain aesthetic markers of Black cultural production and particularity—in fashion, music, and entertainment—are largely divorced from any oppositional politics or practice. We can witness, following Reed, the presence of "otherness" without insurgence or dissent and "a propagation of a model of politics which reinforce[s] over-simplification, the reduction of ideals to banalized objects of immediate consumption." Thus Reed concludes that "opposition increasingly becomes a spectacle in a society organized around reduction of all existence to a series of spectacles."[75]

Narratives of post-1960s declension like this one tend to miss or dismiss many critical historical developments. As Roderick Ferguson has argued, the 1970s and 1980s were also a period in which queer of color– and women of color–led social formations and analytics developed in important ways. They were also a formative period for work around reproductive rights, sex- and gender-based violence, welfare rights, and the politics of intimacy and sexuality more generally.[76] In addition, we must take seriously the intensification of state and non-state violence and repression targeting a broad range of Black insurgent formations across this period.

Yet Reed's broader point about the pluralization and stratification of Black political life during this time and the convergence of corporate-administrative imperatives with the interests of some Black elites requires a serious engagement, and it is a dynamic chronicled by a range of other scholars. Stuart Hall details a similar process in his account of "the end of the innocent notion of the essential black subject" and the weakening of the assumption that race will "guarantee the effectivity of any cultural practice." Like Reed, Hall urges a "recognition of the extraordinary diversity of subjective positions, social experiences and cultural identities which compose the category 'black,'" that forces one to plunge "headlong into the maelstrom of a continuously contingent, unguaranteed, political argument and debate: a critical politics, a politics of criticism."[77]

As Black political elites increasingly became enfolded in the politics of administration and management, and representations of Blackness became unmoored from practices of mass mobilization and demands for the downward distribution of resources, new avenues opened up for mainstream Republicans and Democrats alike to incorporate some registers of Black particularity, subjectivity, and interests into their increasingly conservative political projects. Actors from across the political spectrum became free to reconfigure the aims of civil rights to advance agendas alien to those of the Black freedom movement of the mid-twentieth century and to link the possibilities of Black uplift to conservative policies.

Within the GOP, one example of these dynamics can be traced through the career of former professional football player and Republican congressman Jack Kemp. A hard economic conservative, his co-sponsored Kemp–Roth tax cut on personal income in 1981 was responsible for drastically expanding economic inequality. Yet anticipating the narratives of West and Love, Kemp sought to tie Black advancement to free-market commitments. As George H. W. Bush's secretary of the Department of Housing and Urban Development, he pushed for programs to allow residents of public housing to purchase their own units, for vouchers that would allow poor people to send their children to private schools, and most famously for "enterprise zones" that would give tax incentives to businesses located in inner cities. Convinced that Republicans could foster Black prosperity through conservative means, he met frequently with Black leaders in cities like Chicago, New

York, Philadelphia, and Los Angeles. These policies never fulfilled their stated aspirations or attracted any substantive support among Black voters, but they demonstrate a continuity of attempts within the Republican Party to incorporate some Black presence even as it consolidated its base among conservative white voters through a politics of racial demonization.[78]

In the 1990s, both parties sought to expand their base of white votes through racial demonization on positions related to welfare, immigration, crime, the rollback of affirmative action and bilingual education, militarization and Islamophobia, and anti-discrimination law and policy. Precisely because of the success of these efforts, in the current moment racial politics can no longer be harnessed in the same way to mobilize white voters. Indeed, as the attacks on welfare, affirmative action, and anti-poverty programs in general accelerated in the 1990s, accompanied by a dramatic upturn in Black and brown incarceration rates, the imperative to directly demonize Black and brown subjects shifted. That is, the conservative transformation of the state had succeeded so fully and anti-Blackness had been so thoroughly incorporated into state governance that conservatives were freed to expand various modes of Black incorporation without fear of losing white votes.

In 2000, Republican presidential candidate George W. Bush campaigned on "compassionate conservatism"—a politics that sought to focus positively on the needs of the poor and people of color by connecting small-government and free-market conservative principles to civil rights goals. At the culmination of his party nomination acceptance speech at the Republican National Convention in 2000, he described visiting a juvenile jail in Marlin, Texas, where "one young man, about 15, raised his hand and asked a haunting question: 'What do you think of me?'" Bush reported, "He seemed to be asking, like many Americans who struggle . . . 'Is there hope for me? Do I have a chance?' And, frankly, 'Do you, a white man in a suit, really care what happens to me?'" Bush then went on to describe the philosophy at the heart of compassionate conservatism. "Big government is not the answer. But the alternative to bureaucracy is not indifference. It is to put conservative values and conservative ideas into the thick of the fight for justice and opportunity."[79] Throughout his presidency, Bush returned to this philosophy. Speaking at the national convention of the NAACP in 2006 he celebrated the organization's commitment to the "blessings of liberty and opportunity" and framed a market-based notion of freedom. "Most of your forefathers," he said, "came in chains as property of other people. Today their children and grandchildren have the opportunity to own their own property."[80]

The Republican embrace of neoliberal multiculturalism continued to develop after the Bush years, moving from its prior association with "compassionate conservatism" to the mainstream of conservatism itself. But whereas compassionate conservatism was an ideology aligned at some level with the aims of the civil rights movement, the emphasis now increasingly moved toward narratives of the struggle and triumph of individuals of color as pure affirmation of the marketplace.

It is important to note that the incorporations of Blackness pursued by Republicans in many ways followed a similar process that developed within the Democratic Party, which venerated a type of civil rights universalism even as it pursued policies that widened racial hierarchies. Bill Clinton, for one important example, built his national career on the Democratic Leadership Council strategy of appealing to white reaction. In a moment of violent spectacle early in his 1992 bid for the Democratic nomination for president, Clinton flew to Little Rock on the eve of the New Hampshire primary to personally oversee the death-row execution of Ricky Ray Rector, a mentally disabled Black man. That same election year he scolded rapper Sister Souljah and snubbed Jesse Jackson at the Rainbow Coalition annual convention. Clinton signed historic national anti-crime legislation, contributing greatly to the rise of the modern carceral state, and furthered the dismantling of the U.S. welfare system. These legislative acts, like his campaign actions, were meant to stanch the hemorrhaging of white voters to the GOP.[81]

Yet Clinton evinced another, seemingly opposite political strategy throughout, which was to demonstrate an ease and facility with Black America. This Clinton was often seen on the golf course with his friend Vernon Jordan, a Revlon executive. He spoke frankly about racism. On a historic trip to Africa, he apologized for slavery. And famously, during his impeachment for lying about an extramarital affair with a White House intern, Toni Morrison called him "our first black president."[82]

While seemingly in contradiction, these two sides to Clinton demonstrate a deeper shift in the main currents of elite U.S. politics that can be seen at work in both parties: a cultural celebration of Black America that performs moral authority, a narrative of overcoming, and a commitment to individual freedom that is increasingly delinked from the historic imperatives of racial justice and material redistribution; and an anti-statist, pro-market, and anti-egalitarian politics that produces profound racial inequality. As Michelle Alexander explained in a 2016 article in *The Nation*, "Clinton mastered the art of sending mixed cultural messages, appealing to African Americans by belting out 'Lift Every Voice and Sing' in black churches, while at the same time signaling to poor and working-class whites that he was willing to be tougher on black communities than Republicans had been."[83]

The synthesis of these forces was nowhere more visible than at a Rose Garden press conference in 1996 where Clinton signed the legislation eviscerating federally funded welfare programs and replacing a major pillar of state-sponsored income support with various "workfare" and even marriage-promotion programs.[84] Clinton signed the bill flanked by two Black women who had been recipients of the Aid to Families with Dependent Children program he was abolishing, their appearance suggesting that he was ending the program in their name and in their interests. In his short remarks at the bill's signing, he neither mentioned their names nor described their experiences.[85] Their sole purpose was to serve as a symbolic backdrop.

By Obama's election in 2008, the bipartisan project to dismantle welfare, abolish affirmative action and school desegregation, weaken anti-discrimination protections, militarize immigration policy, and fully realize the prison–industrial complex had largely been completed. Coupled with the long-term decline of antiracist social movements, these developments shifted the terrain of contemporary racial politics. Obama's 2008 campaign traded continually on the cultural significance of his Blackness as a symbol of civil rights achievement specifically and of American exceptionalism more generally. From his victory speech following the Iowa caucuses where he insisted that "they said this day would never come" to the Democratic National Committee's declaration of "I Have a Dream Day" on the day of his nomination in Denver, the Obama campaign suggestively associated the candidate with civil rights achievements in powerful ways without making substantive links to policy prescriptions aimed at the advancement of the Black freedom struggle.[86]

When we situate the ascent of Alan West, Mia Love, Tim Scott, and other contemporary conservatives of color within this longer history, their appeal to a deeply conservative base of white voters no longer seems so peculiar. Like Obama and Booker, they frame their narratives of Black uplift and the legacies of civil rights in the same terms of American exceptionalism, market freedoms, and anti-statism that ironically once animated an explicitly racist political discourse.

In addition, Blackness still often embodies and expresses excess and danger in this discourse. Consider Michelle Obama's speech to the graduating class of Martin Luther King Jr. Preparatory High School in Chicago in 2015, in which she described "the story of that quiet majority of good folks—families like mine and young people like all of you who face real challenges but make good choices every single day."[87] Like the Silent Majority, this "quiet majority of good folks," defined by their cultural attributes, upright decisions, and moral values, is implicitly constructed in contrast to an immoral and lawless racially coded other, whose poor choices and diminished values make them culpable in their own degradation. Black incorporation here offers a reformulation and modest desegregation in the membership of a racially stratified populace while still retaining its core elements: long-standing articulations of American cultural superiority, valorization of individual freedoms, and the denigration of bad subjects.

"It Turned Me into a Fighter"

On a Tuesday morning in early December 2017, hundreds of scholars and staffers at the Heritage Foundation were addressed for the first time by their newly appointed president. Seven months earlier, the foundation's twenty-two-member board had unanimously called for the resignation of Jim DeMint, the former South Carolina senator and Tea Party favorite whose appointment in 2013 as Heritage president was viewed as an effort to put the prestigious think tank closer in touch with the grassroots conservative mobilizations that were sweeping the nation. But after four years, the board and others within the foundation became increasingly concerned that DeMint was both mismanaging the organization and neglecting its long-standing focus on conservative intellectual development and policy formation.[88]

Following a months-long search, the foundation's board turned to one of its own to right the ship. Kay Coles James had been a significant player in the conservative movement for decades.[89] In the early 1990s she served as senior vice president of the conservative Christian Family Research Council, and in the late 1990s she was a dean at Regent University, an evangelical institution founded by Pat Robertson that has trained hundreds of conservative political leaders.[90] She also held appointments in the presidential administrations of Ronald Reagan and George H. W. Bush, and under George W. Bush she directed the Office of Personnel Management. The Bush administration would come to employ more than 150 Regent University graduates during her tenure.[91] Together with former Reagan staffer Ed Meese, she led Trump's transition team for three major federal administrative offices.[92]

James had also been a trustee of the Heritage Foundation since 2005 and was chairing the search for the new president. She was, in this sense, the consummate insider's candidate, the grownup brought in to restore order and recommit Heritage to its mission. In a statement released to Heritage supporters at the time of her appointment, James promised: "You have my commitment: Heritage is safe with me. I'm in awe of this treasure you've built, and I pledge to you that I will protect it and grow it with the greatest care possible."[93]

James, the preeminent conservative movement builder, is also a Black woman. And like West, Love, and Scott, she does not deploy her racialized and gendered experiences to counsel Black people to behave differently, but instead seeks to assert the deep resonance between conservative ideals and Black well-being. A graduate of the historically Black Hampton University, she also founded and presides over the Gloucester Institute, an organization that trains young Black leaders in conservative ideals through fellowships, trainings, and other leadership-development programs.[94] As a Heritage trustee she wrote a commentary for the foundation's website, *The Daily Signal*, titled "I'm an African-American Woman: Here's My Advice to Conservatives Wooing My Community." Suggesting that a commitment to Black well-being and a commitment to "social justice" should be central to conservative politics, she insists: "It's not OK that black kids aren't getting the very best education possible. It's not OK that black adults are out of work and unable to pursue their dreams. It's not OK that black families are homeless. It's not OK that black seniors live in fear for what tomorrow may bring. And it's not OK that so many consultants and pundits would rather play politics than help save my people."[95] She told Heritage employees when her appointment was announced that "these problems can be found everywhere that liberalism has left its devastating mark. In inner cities. In Appalachia. In the Rust Belt. And in far too many white, brown, and black communities from coast to coast."[96]

James also draws on her experiences facing discrimination growing up in segregated neighborhoods and schools in Richmond, Virginia, to bolster her credentials as a fighter for conservative causes. She told Heritage employees on her first day about her experiences walking down the hall in integrated school as classmates kicked her, called her names, and stuck her with pins. "It turned me into a fighter," she said, a commitment she would use to guide the foundation.

In an interview two months later on Breitbart Radio, following her appearance at the 2018 CPAC, she explained why she had no hesitation in going to college campuses and other perceived bastions of liberalism and winning over students to the principles and commitments of conservative ideas. "Growing up as a black conservative, pro-life, evangelical . . . I know what it feels like to be ostracized . . . [and] to have people hate you because of your positions and what you believe. So I'm truly not intimidated by any of that."[97] At a time when many conservatives imagine themselves bravely defying the scorn of liberal and centrist elites, narratives like James's become a generative source of identification and assurance.

Kay Coles James's ascent to the one of the most important and prestigious positions in the conservative movement demonstrates many of the central ideas explored in this chapter. At a time of growing precarity and vulnerability for many white households, figures like James, Love, West, and Scott become the idealized subjects of the marketized and militarized nation, continually testifying to its exceptional qualities at a time of crisis. They exemplify important changes in the ways race is being deployed within dominant modes of neoliberal governance and electoral politics, as well as the shaping of popular consent under conditions of growing precarity. As we will see in the next chapter, these forms of racial incorporation have even moved beyond the GOP and conservative think tanks to the shoals of the far right.

4

"A BROWN BROTHER FOR DONALD TRUMP"

The Multiculturalism of the Far Right

• • •

In the wake of Donald Trump's presidential inauguration in 2017, far-right and white-nationalist groups organized militant pro-Trump and "free speech" rallies in cities around the United States. A few figures in this scene became celebrities in alt-right circles for bloodying counter-protesters who came to oppose them. Some were open white supremacists like Identity Evropa's Nathan Damigo or Kyle "Based Stickman" Chapman. Among the most notorious of them, though, was a brawler who was neither a member of a white-supremacist group nor even white. Rather, he was a Samoan with an ironic nickname: Tusitala "Tiny" Toese. How did this native Pacific Islander become, in his words, a "brown brother for Donald Trump," and why was he so enthusiastically embraced by the far right? Actually, Tiny's story is not unique. On the contemporary far right we find an increasing presence of people of color and even a celebration of non-white ethnicity and culture. There is a growing, tangled relationship between renewed forms of authoritarian nationalism and a masculinized version of multiculturalism, one that selectively incorporates some people of color into a nationalist framework.

The emergent and contradictory phenomenon we examine in this chapter blurs the putative distinction between an exclusionary racial nationalism and an inclusionary civic nationalism made by scholars of race in U.S. political history such as Rogers Smith and Gary Gerstle.[1] Reaching back to the nation's founding, it is clear that the form of white supremacy peculiar to the United States is oriented not simply toward commitments to racial purity and stock but also toward a vision of a multiracial nation premised on racial hierarchy and white domination. This vision, paradoxically, depends on the visibility and participation of non-white racialized subjects as it advances forms of authoritarianism and exclusion that facilitate racist attacks on specific groups today: Muslims, undocumented immigrants, Black Lives Matter activists, and the Black and brown poor more generally.

In explicating the complicated dynamics of race within the far right, we do not seek to downplay the hard kernel of white supremacy at its heart. Instead, we aim to demonstrate how a logic of multiculturalism has served to reproduce white nationalism. The presence of some people of color within the alt-right, alt-lite, and Trumpist folds does not diminish or qualify the racist commitments of these efforts. Paradoxically, the incorporation of people of color by the far right makes white supremacy a more durable force. Gender and sexuality are always fundamental to the production of far-right politics, working as a fulcrum for these racially transpositive politics. Performed as patriarchal traditionalism, online ultra-misogyny, or street-brawling bravado, masculinity bridges racial difference for populist, fascist, and even white-nationalist politics.

The contemporary far right is diverse and under continual renovation, particularly in regard to race. Seen one way, the far right's definitional instability makes it difficult to analyze in a concrete fashion. But we argue that it is precisely this racial ambiguity that generates power and meaning for this broad formation. Disavowal of open white supremacy allows the far right to draw in more recruits and allows participants a certain racial innocence—a plausible deniability of open racism. Moreover, it allows a deepening commitment to racialized concepts that can, on their face, be denied to be racist. And finally, we argue, it is often the powerful symbolism of subaltern figures that gives the far right some of its constitutive force. The uncertain racial boundaries of the far right allow its participants to draw from racial narratives about people of color to bolster certain forms of whiteness, particularly through nationalism and gender. Thus while the use of the terms alt-right and alt-lite today are meant to distinguish between the embrace of open white racism on the one hand and the rejection of racial identitarianism on the other, this border cannot withstand close scrutiny. This racially protean character of the far right is precisely the quality that ultimately bolsters white supremacy.

Steve Bannon: White Nationalism versus Economic Nationalism

In August 2017, following a Unite the Right rally in Charlottesville, Virginia, at which an antiracist activist was killed by a neofascist, Trump's chief strategist, Steve Bannon, made a surprising statement: "Ethno-nationalism—it's losers. It's a fringe element. I think the media plays it up too much, and we gotta help crush it. These guys are a collection of clowns."[2] Bannon's hard dismissal of the white supremacists at the forefront of the Charlottesville demonstrations seems surprising. Bannon, after all, launched himself into the national spotlight and Trump's inner circle while serving as the executive editor of Breitbart News, a venue he described as the "platform for the Alt-Right." Bannon extolled openly racist tracts such as *The Camp of the Saints* (*Le camp des saints*), an apocalyptic French novel written in 1973 by Jean Raspail that portrayed the fall of Western Europe and ultimately all so-called white nations at the hands of a massive tide of immigrants from the Global South.[3] Bannon's appointment to the White House was celebrated by white supremacists, including former Ku Klux Klan grand wizard David Duke, who described his appointment as "excellent," anticipating that Bannon was "basically creating the ideological aspects of where we're going."[4]

Together with senior adviser Stephen Miller and Attorney General Jeff Sessions, Bannon represented the racist, nativist, and populist wing of the Trump White House and was a key figure in the Trump administration's early attempts to enact a travel ban targeting visitors to the United States from Muslim-majority countries and to "build a wall" on the U.S. border with Mexico.

Yet in response to a question about popular perception of him as a white nationalist, Bannon told the *New York Times* in November 2017, "The people who have been most affected negatively by globalism in this country are the working-class Hispanics and blacks in this country, which has really taken opportunities away. That is why," he went on, "if you start bringing jobs back to the Midwest, if you stop illegal immigration—I've said this from day one in our movement—when we get to 25 and 30 percent of the black working class and the Hispanic working class voting for us, we will have a realignment like 1932."[5]

Soon after the *New York Times* interview, Bannon spoke at a meeting of the South Carolina Black Chamber of Commerce to elaborate his idea of economic nationalism. Linking racial exclusion to economic exclusion, Bannon told his audience, "Minority entrepreneurs are the biggest customers of community banks. And you know why they didn't get recapitalized? Because nobody cares. When it comes time to make the deals, you're not in the room."[6] Bannon also spoke to the Washington, D.C.–based conservative organization Black Americans for a Better Future, where he told his audience, "The central part of economic nationalism depends upon you. It depends upon us empowering the black and Hispanic entrepreneurial community with one thing: Access to capital." Reynard Jackson, founder of the group, said in an interview about Bannon afterward, "If you were Stevie Wonder, being blind, and you could sit and talk with Steve and didn't know his color, you would swear he's from the black community because of his understanding of the dynamic, the business and community dynamic."[7]

But is economic nationalism actually the repudiation of white nationalism that Bannon claims it is? There are distinct principles shared by both positions, such as opposition to immigration and opposition to free trade, and then there are the broader ideas that pervade both Bannon's politics and those of white nationalists: a commitment to "Western values and culture" that is stridently anti-Islam and anti-Chinese, a fear that majority-white countries will be overwhelmed and destroyed by invaders from the Global South, and an anti-"globalism" that carries the strong taint of anti-Semitism.

Yet the xenophobia, anti-Islamic bigotry, and anti-Semitism expressed or implied by economic nationalism is not softened by a domestic multiracial embrace but actually bolstered by it. As Bannon explains it, any future electoral calculation for his political vision in a multiracial polity depends on inclusion of Black and Hispanic citizens. But such inclusion does other work here as well. Exclusion and economic oppression as he explains them are not the result of institutional racism in the United States but rather of "globalism" and illegal immigration. Bannon's appeal to "the working-class Hispanics and blacks in this country" provides moral underpinning to his claims that immigration (both authorized and unauthorized) destroys jobs and that free-trade agreements favor the rich over everyone else. Thus he describes a kind of class solidarity and interest quite different from that of neoliberal multiculturalists, and this assemblage of Black and Latino/a citizens along with whites gives his proposed coalition historic significance. "The globalists gutted the American working class and created a middle class in Asia. The issue now is about Americans looking to not get fucked over. If [the Trump White House delivers], we'll get 60 percent of the white vote, and 40 percent of the black and Hispanic vote, and we'll govern for fifty years."[8] Here is a portrait of American national identity whose contours are enhanced by counterposing a multiracial working class within against antagonistic global forces without. To reduce this identity to white racial terms alone would be to diminish its identificatory power.

Racial Transposition on the Far Right

The tendency to imagine the contemporary far right as functioning outside the boundaries of U.S. liberalism and pluralism (or perhaps, more specifically, as a backlash against the inclusionary commitments of the civic-nationalist tradition) misses the dynamic play between American civic nationalism and white-racial nationalism. The contemporary far right in the United States demonstrates the ways that the politically inclusionary symbols, claims, and logics of civic nationalism draw on the culturally hierarchical commitments of racial nationalism. Civic and racial nationalism here are more productively understood as mutually constitutive. The Trump campaign's claims, in Nixonian tones, to speak for the Silent Majority or Middle America, to enforce law and order, and to build a border wall are all inexorably tied to an imagining of the United States as a white, colonial nation. But explicit calls to defend the white race are too concrete and abandon the fantasy of American universalism on which the national project depends. Although this unapologetically closed vision of national identity has been an enduring presence in U.S. political history, it has always been contested. An open commitment to white supremacy abandons many of the meanings invested in American national identity that valorize and legitimate the exceptional qualities and standing of the nation. These meanings have diverse historical touchstones; they are evident in the texts of the Declaration of Independence and the Constitution, icons such as the Statue of Liberty and the Lincoln Memorial, and moments of national sacrifice that include the American Revolution, the Civil War, and World War II. Such markers of American identity can be and have been interpreted in ways that secure white racial dominance, but only by evasion. The broad ideals that make up American exceptionalism must deny racial distinction in order to have resonance. In this sense, racialized civic nationalism imagines national subjects not through biological fantasies of whiteness but as people who aspire to the ideals of the nation through competition in the marketplace, shared civic values, respect for law, militarism, and individual freedom.

The political theorist Michael Rogin wrote that "whereas the political Declaration of Independence made an anticolonial revolution in the name of the equality of all men, the declaration of cultural independence [from the strictures of the Old World] emerged not to free oppressed folk but to constitute national identity out of their subjugation." Rogin argued that while "white supremacy, white over black and red, was the content of this national culture," "its form was black and red over white, blacking up and Indianization."[9] Thus, American nationalists can claim to stand for deportation of the undocumented, the construction of a border wall, increased policing in poor communities, and a

Muslim ban in the name of an America that is multiracial, egalitarian, and freedom loving. Emphasizing cultural notions of nationalism over explicit references to race allows for the use of antiracist language to work on behalf of white nationalism.

Scholars such as Richard Slotkin and Philip Deloria have demonstrated that an emergent American identity from the seventeenth through the twentieth centuries depended on "playing Indian"— a kind of racialized cross-dressing that selectively incorporated characteristics attributed to indigenous people, such as incorruptability, aversion to foreign rule, autonomy, ferocity, and a tie to the natural world.[10] The mythologization of Native people was expressed in place-names, on coins, in the literature of James Fenimore Cooper, in John Filson's Daniel Boone dime novels, which featured a racially cross-dressing settler hero, and even in historian Frederick Jackson Turner's famous thesis on the relationship between Indian identification and the durability of American democratic institutions.[11] Such myths did not run counter to the imperatives of settler colonialism. Indeed, they were often intertwined with the belief that Euro-Americans were destined to conquer and rule North America.

Similarly, the enslavement of Africans and the theft of Black labor was fundamental to the making of the American nation not just materially but politically and culturally. Toni Morrison and James Baldwin have argued that the very meanings of white American freedom and progress have rested on the uses and abuses of Blackness, in texts that range from the Declaration of Independence to the writings of Norman Mailer, from blackface minstrelsy through jazz to hip hop. This relationship of "love and theft," as Eric Lott called it, demonstrates the degree to which any meaningful notion of American national identity in the world's "first new nation" requires racialized amalgamation and symbolic borrowing.[12] As one member of the neo-Nazi internet forum Stormfront posted its message board: "I sometimes listen to Bob Marley and when he sings about black liberation I pretend he is singing about white liberation instead."[13]

Historian Carroll Smith-Rosenberg described the production of *homo nationalis* in early American history in which a secure national subjectivity of white men was achieved in a triangulated relationship of selective incorporation and abjection with "the white middle-class woman, the American Indian warrior, and the enslaved African American." As she put it, "internal contradictions, rejected or hated aspects of the subject, are projected outward onto negatively constructed others who exist in 'Manichaean' opposition to a now empowered and purified self, serving as foils against which the uncertain subject is consolidated and mobilized. At the same time, more positive aspects of those others may be appropriated in a process we might call selective identification or symbiosis."[14]

A related claim could be made today about the reproduction of a historically racialized national identity in an increasingly multicultural society. On the contemporary far right we can see both the construction of negative racialized others and selective identification of aspects of figures of color that shore up the national subject, particularly in regard to gender. To be sure, the contemporary groups that explicitly champion a specifically white racial-nationalist framework reject any association with people of color. For example, Richard Spencer, who coined the term "alt-right" and is president of the white-supremacist National Policy Institute, has called for "an ethno-state that would be a gathering point for all Europeans." The "race realist" journal *American Renaissance*, the neo-Nazi internet forum Stormfront, and other racists associated with the alt-right similarly envision a "pure" white racial polity. These groups parallel the rise of more openly racist formations in Europe built on explicit visions of ethnonationalism.

By contrast, several far-right formations that have accompanied Trump's rise have integrated civic-nationalist and racial-nationalist discourses in ways that have openly facilitated the participation of some people of color in these movements. In this context, calls to defend "civilization," "culture," "the West," or (Bannon's oft-deployed term) "Judeo-Christian values" can be used to legitimate and reproduce a nationalist project that is at once inclusionary and hierarchical. It creates room for political actors on the far right to enlist some people of color, or at least to selectively appropriate language and symbols associated with multiculturalism. In the next section we turn to various instances of the multicultural far right at work. As we will see, its rising tide draws on diverse formulas of race, gender, class, and nation to generate an authoritarian nationalist politics.

"If Bill Clinton Can Do Mass Incarceration, We Can Do Mass Deportation!"

Just as Steve Bannon used Black and Latino/a citizens to provide moral authority for his economic nationalism, the Trump campaign situated African Americans symbolically against immigrants from Latin America. In this expression of multicultural right-wing populism, African Americans are held up as law-abiding citizens preyed upon by undocumented immigrants—even through the use of the same scripts of criminality and incorrigibility that have fueled Black mass incarceration. Making Black Americans victims of immigration serves to strengthen the case for deportation and border security in a way that simple race rhetoric could not.

The most exemplary figures of this trope were the African American video bloggers Lynnette Hardaway and Rochelle Richardson, a.k.a. Diamond and Silk. Fixtures on the campaign trail as the "Stump for Trump Girls," Hardaway and Richardson were popular at rallies, even in the Deep South, where Trump voters' racial animus was particularly pronounced.

As African Americans, Diamond and Silk were uniquely positioned both to claim color blindness to a white Mississippian audience and then to make a veiled criticism of the Black Lives Matter movement. As a kind of talisman used to repel charges of racism among Trump supporters, the duo could safely attack Black activism on their behalf. For example, at a nearly all-white rally of fifteen thousand people in Biloxi, Mississippi, in January 2016, the pair told a cheering crowd, "That's right baby, we're stumpin' for Trump up in here . . . and listen, let me tell you something. There is only one race! That's right. And that's the human race. And all of our lives matter in this room!" During his own speech at the rally, Trump said he felt "surrounded by love" and then brought Diamond and Silk onstage for a second time to stand with him. Referring to Obama, Hardaway shouted to the roaring crowd, "This time, we're going to have real change!" Finally, in a signature campaign gesture meant to invoke the thrill of assaults on Black demonstrators these rallies became known for, Trump stood next to Diamond and Silk and asked the crowd, "Do we have a protester available? . . . It would be good television."[15] In this performance, as in others, the embrace of rightwing nativist African Americans was tied directly to an attack on Black protestors.

One of the most frequently repeated Diamond and Silk themes during the campaign was the unfair criminalization of Black people in contrast to the supposed real criminality of the undocumented. At an "America First" rally outside the Republican National Convention in July 2016, Diamond and Silk told the crowd, "If we go to someone's house uninvited, and we go right up in their house, they call that breaking and entering! It's just wrong to go into someone's house and take their things!" Depicting undocumented immigrants as burglars makes law-abiding African Americans members of the American household. Yet here again, theirs is not a colorblind claim about American citizenship. It is the articulation of a Black subaltern position that authorizes a harsh anti-immigrant stance. "If Bill Clinton can do mass incarceration," they say on one of their YouTube videos, "we can do mass deportation!"[16]

The Trump campaign continually pushed the notion that undocumented immigrants endanger both the lives and livelihoods of Black Americans. During the Republican primaries, the campaign began running a television spot about Jamiel Shaw Jr., a Black high school student and professional football hopeful who had been murdered by an undocumented immigrant in 2008. From the stage on the first night of the Republican National Convention, Jamiel Shaw Sr. addressed the audience to say that his son had been killed because he was Black. Here again, anti-immigrant nativism was expressed as a form of antiracist nationalism. After describing the gruesome details of his son's murder in a primetime speaking slot, Jamiel Shaw Sr. said, "For two weeks, local politicians supported us. And every black politician in L.A. did too. . . . Two weeks later, everything changed. We learned that the killer was an illegal alien gangbanger from Mexico. Released from jail on a deportation hold, three gun charges, and an assault and battery on a police officer. And the politicians disappeared. . . . It was also proved that the killer's gang targeted black males. You'd think Obama cared, and black lives mattered. No. . . . Only Trump called me on the phone one day to see how I was doing. Only Trump will stand against terrorists and end illegal immigration. The wall. . . . Build the wall."[17]

Shaw's status as an African American is central to the arguments he makes against undocumented immigrants and for his support for Trump. In Shaw Sr.'s story, his son is targeted because he is Black. And yet neither a Black social movement nor Black elected officials will support him, because, Shaw implies, they do not want to alienate Latino/a constituents. For Shaw, only Trump can offer protection to Black people in the American nation. We can see here how Blackness is used to reinforce the xenophobic nationalism of the Trump campaign but in a way that simultaneously discredits Black political agency.

It is important to remember that Shaw's and Diamond and Silk's nativist politics do not represent the broader contours of African American political opinion related to immigration. A 2018 poll found African American respondents opposed Trump's "border wall" by a margin of 87 to 13 percent, higher than the rate of 71 to 25 percent among Latino/a respondents.[18] While other surveys have recorded more ambivalent attitudes, the efforts to incorporate African American voters and political blocs into restrictionist formations has largely been a failure.[19] Immigration restrictionist groups like the Federation for American Immigration Reform (FAIR) have attempted to organize "independent" Black formations to make the claim that immigration restriction is a top civil rights and economic justice issue for African Americans.[20] These groups rarely lasted more than a few months or involved more than a handful of spokespersons.[21]

Shaw and Diamond and Silk, by contrast, emerged independent of mainstream restrictionist formations. But the dynamic goes deeper. Black nativism has a narrow but distinct legacy, stretching back from the Black-led boycott of Korean groceries in New York

City in the 1990s to tensions between Black citizenship and immigrant incorporation at the turn of the twentieth century—tensions that, as political scientist Claire Jean Kim has demonstrated, ultimately reward white supremacy.[22]

Race, Class, and Nation: Uncle Chang and Little Britney

Far-right multiculturalism has also been used to connect Trumpism to the online world of the alt-right. For one example, in early January 2017, actor Shia LaBeouf opened his "He Will Not Divide Us" (HWNDU) livestream exhibit at the Museum of the Moving Image in New York City. Set up in response to Trump's inauguration, the interactive exhibit was meant to be an open invitation for anyone who wished to register his or her opposition to the new president. Soon after the exhibit was opened, however, it became a target for far-right counterpoint. On January 31, a young Asian American man who later adopted the *nom de internet* "Uncle Chang" delivered a short monologue at HWNDU. Saying "This is why you lost," Uncle Chang argued to the liberal-leaning HWNDU audience that Hillary Clinton was defeated because liberal voters embraced "identity politics" and treated Asian Americans as "voting blocs instead of people." After stating that he came from a working-class family, Uncle Chang declared, "This is why I voted for Trump. Fuck you. Suck my big Asian cock. . . . If I'm a Nazi then Sieg Heil, motherfucker!"[23]

Uncle Chang came back to the HWNDU livestream three days later, this time with a multiracial group of supporters around him to more fully explain why Democrats had lost the 2016 presidential election. This second video was edited and uploaded to the website of former Breitbart tech editor and alt-lite media provocateur Milo Yiannopoulos, where it quickly garnered tens of millions of views. In the second video, Uncle Chang further elaborates his account. "You lost because you told the poor, white, working-class families in rural Pennsylvania, Wisconsin, and Michigan that they were the privileged ones. That despite losing their jobs, despite their factories shipping to China and Mexico, and despite barely being able to put food on the table, that they were privileged ones because of the color of their skin. I come from a working-class family and let me tell you, the struggle doesn't discriminate. Working-class parents work their hands to the bone in the hopes that their children will have better lives than them. When their jobs get shipped overseas, so do their hopes and dreams." He went on, "They're not privileged. You're privileged. You sit in your big comfy chairs in your fancy offices up in the ivory towers of university sociology departments and you expect us to give two shits and a fuck about your identity politics? The first thing we think of when we wake up isn't intersectional transfeminism. It's whether or not we'll be able to make this month's rent. It's whether or not our bronze-tier Obamacare plan will cover little Britney's weird cough. Britney is sick. So sick. And we don't know what's wrong with her. It might be because we don't have enough money. We can only afford to feed her cold chicken tendies."[24]

At one level, Uncle Chang's argument is the same as that of color-blind conservatives: Trump supporters care about economics, not race, and liberals see everything in racial terms, thereby reducing individuals to group status. But the melodramatic affective work here is more complex and more powerful. For Uncle Chang, not only is "identity politics" illegitimate, but liberals who subscribe to them are blinded to the social pain he depicts. Little Britney is "so sick," and her "weird cough" may not be covered under the health-care plan that liberals so love. Indeed, there isn't even an available energy source to heat her chicken tendies.

Like Tiny Tim in Dickens's *A Christmas Carol*, little Britney has an unspecified disease, but one that remains untreatable "if," as the Ghost of Christmas Present puts it, "these shadows remain unaltered" and the hearts of the privileged remain unmoved by suffering.[25] But who is Britney? A relative of Uncle Chang? A neighbor? A member of one of "the poor, white, working class families in rural Pennsylvania, Wisconsin, and Michigan" that he describes? Her identity is never made clear except as a child marked by economic oppression, as an excluded figure that liberals cannot even see. She stands in as a synecdoche for the vulnerable working-class base of Trump support for whom Uncle Chang claims to speak.

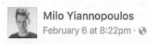

Milo Yiannopoulos
February 6 at 8:22pm · 🌐

THIS

ASIAN TRUMP SUPPORTER CRUSHES LIBERALS AND IDENTITY POLITICS

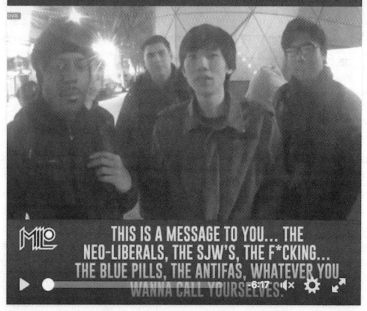

THIS IS A MESSAGE TO YOU... THE
NEO-LIBERALS, THE SJW'S, THE F*CKING...
THE BLUE PILLS, THE ANTIFAS, WHATEVER YOU
WANNA CALL YOURSELVES.

▶ ●   6:17 ◀× ⚙ ↗

16M Views

👍 Like   💬 Comment   ↪ Share   </> Embed   📷 ▾

👍😮🐨 Paul Pk Kim, Mark Seaquist and 208K others   Top Comments ▾

296,119 shares   22K Comments

Milo Yiannopoulos social-media posting titled "Asian Trump Supporter Crushes Liberals and Identity Politics," February 6, 2017. The clip referenced in the posting was recorded by Uncle Chang at the *He Will Not Divide Us* livestream exhibit at the Museum of the Moving Image in New York City, February 3, 2017.

In a later interview posted to YouTube, Uncle Chang revealed that he is a computer science student at New York University, the son of Chinese immigrants, and a native of Brooklyn. As Uncle Chang describes it, working-class identity and nationalism animate his support for Trump. Yet central to these politics are their proximity to a whiteness that he wants to defend. He told the online Asian American youth magazine *Nextshark*, "Right now, in the social climate, straight white men are on the bottom. Anyone above them can talk trash about them and it's socially acceptable. That's what I don't like. That's not equality. That's definitely not the equality that I was raised with."[26] His strong identification with nation and class need not, in itself, be raced. Yet it is through white grievance that he chooses to express this identification.

Here, then, is how multicultural far-right logic works in the case of Uncle Chang: he claims an identity that is non-white, meant to make liberalism ring hollow by virtue of his racial positioning ("You're the real racist ones," he tells Clinton supporters). He then goes on to affirm working-class identity and U.S. patriotism against the race-obsessed liberalism he attacks. Yet he ultimately returns to defend white men—demonstrating that race and gender remain the ultimate mediators of far-right identity. "Uncle Chang" is a term meant to denote subservience to the white race. Even if meant ironically, it underscores the centrality of racial hierarchies to his message and persona. Nothing about the far right's racist commitments is disrupted here. Rather, they are secured by the speaker's Chinese American identity.

Multicultural Masculinity and the Protofascist Right

Perhaps the least likely place one would expect to find far-right multiculturalism would be in its most violent spaces. During and after the 2016 Trump campaign, militant right-wing street demonstrations became increasingly frequent. White-nationalist and openly fascist organizations acted as the advance guard of pro-Trump and "free speech" demonstrations, including Identity Evropa, the Traditional Workers Party, the League of the South, and Ku Klux Klan groups. The man who smashed a car into a

crowd of antiracists, killing Heather Heyer at the Charlottesville Unite the Right rally, was a member of the fascist National
Vanguard.[27]

Yet one of the most notorious streetfighters to emerge from
this milieu is not a white supremacist but a Samoan who is a self-
proclaimed antiracist and former Trump opponent. Tiny Toese,
introduced at the beginning of this chapter, considered Trump
supporters to be racists worthy of attack during the 2016 campaign. "I'd drive around and beat them up," he says, or watch
online videos of Trump supporters getting assaulted. "It made
me happy. F—in' racists getting beaten up," he said.[28] One day,
Toese came across a video of alt-right persona and leader of the
group Patriot Prayer, Joey Gibson, who talked about love and
unity. Toese said this made him question his assumptions. Toese
reached out to Gibson, who is Japanese American, and through
him met other alt-right activists, began attending "free speech"
rallies, and getting into violent altercations with antifascists.

In a speech he gave at a Patriot Prayer "freedom rally" in
Seattle in August 2017, Toese recounted his personal efforts coming to terms with the perceived racism of the Trump campaign
and the patriot movement and his identity as a person of color.
He described his first experience with Patriot Prayer—a road trip
from Portland to a rally in Berkeley—and explained, "it was just
the Brown guy in the car [himself], and three white dudes." As the
trip began he found himself thinking that "these guys are really
racist." But when they stopped to eat along the way, he continued,
they encountered an older Latino man with a flat tire. He thought,
"let me see if these white dudes are really racist . . . if they're going
to go help, or if they're going to leave the guy there." When one
of the others in the car insisted on helping the motorist, Toese
explained, he "became more confused. Are they really racist or
not?" This conversion experience on the road to Damascus—or
rather Berkeley—released him to join confrontations with Antifa
protesters, whom he now saw as the real aggressors.[29]

When Toese and other Patriot Prayer members went to Evergreen University in Olympia, Washington, that summer to confront

antiracist student protesters, they posted a photo on social media with the title "White Supremacists Coming to Evergreen State. Patriot Prayer—A Racist Group That Accepts Members of All Races." The title, meant to be facetious, suggested that by definition, a group that included people of color could not be racist. The accompanying photo showed Toese and four others wearing shirts that read "ISIS Hunting Permit." Here, a reference to civic nationalism (a group that "accepts members of all races") is merged explicitly with racial nationalism (an open celebration of anti-Islamic violence).

Toese's embrace of the far right has been returned by a burgeoning scene that is clearly infatuated with the presence of an American Samoan streetfighter. But is not merely the "Antifa Destroyer's" size and pugilism that alt-righters love. Toese also quite literally performs non-white masculinity. At a Patriot Prayer rally in downtown Portland on June 4, 2017, he led participants in the Siva Tau haka, a Samoan war dance.

The rally occurred just a week after avowed white supremacist Jeremy Christian stabbed two people to death and severely injured a third who had intervened to stop Christian from threatening two young Muslim women on the Portland Max train. The trauma of the attack brought thousands of people out to the streets to oppose the "Trump Free Speech Rally" that organizer Joey Gibson insisted on holding.

But why would far-right protesters find Toese's haka ritual so compelling? The cultural anthropologist Brendan Hokowhitu has argued that the performance of the haka in popular culture evokes heteropatriarchal nationalism in settler-colonial contexts even while maintaining racial difference and hierarchy.[30] Here a colonial subject of a U.S. territory proclaims his allegiance to American freedom before leading white members of the colonizing nation in a traditional war dance at the rally. The demonstrators, surrounded by a much larger number of Portlanders outraged that such a rally would take place mere days after a white-supremacist double murder in their city, clearly revel in the martial ritual as they prepare to confront their opponents on the streets.

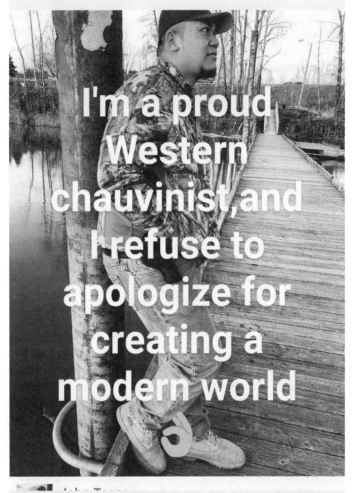

I'm a proud Western chauvinist, and I refuse to apologize for creating a modern world

 **Facebook** INSTALLED   Open

Screenshot of meme posted on Tiny Toese's Facebook page featuring a version of the slogan of the far-right men's group the Proud Boys. The hand gesture below the caption has been appropriated by the alt-right.

Yet for all of his Samoan gestures to multiracial inclusion on the right, Toese, like Uncle Chang, explicitly defends white people, whom he sees as under siege. In one of his Facebook livestreams from an "It's Okay to Be White" rally on an overpass bridge outside Portland, Toese wears the iconic white-nationalist Pepe the Frog mask and tells viewers, "A lot of people don't know but if you really look at it, white people are under attack in this country. If it's okay to be black, if it's okay to be brown, then it's okay to be white too."[31] The "It's Okay to Be White" slogan, meant to sound benign, was actually hatched by neo-Nazis, spread virally across social media and onto posters on campuses across the country, and finally endorsed by conservative political commentator Tucker Carlson on Fox News in late 2017.

Toese's comrade Joey Gibson also exemplifies the relationship between a racially inclusionary authoritarian nationalism and the far right, as discussed in this book's Introduction. The confrontational rallies he has organized under the names Patriot Prayer and Warriors for Freedom in Portland, Oregon, and Vancouver, Washington, as well as the one he attempted in San Francisco, have drawn openly white-nationalist groups such as Identity Evropa and have featured white-supremacist speakers such as Tim Gionet (aka "Baked Alaska"). Gibson has frequently denounced white supremacists and Nazis (even as they populate his rallies), yet he glorifies violent street confrontations with leftwing radicals and antifascists in defense of Trump and free speech.

Violent masculinity is the identity and practice that brings together explicit racists with fascist people of color. Much of what is now called the alt-right came out of the men's-rights and male-supremacy movements that have proliferated in the last few years among young men, particularly in online imageboard communities such as 4chan and 8chan. As this culture developed, many of its proponents were increasingly drawn to white-supremacist groups.[32] The most prominent men's-rights proponent on the right is media figure Gavin McInnes, co-founder of *Vice* magazine and founder of a group called the Proud Boys, a "pro-Western fraternal organization." Indeed, even the term McInnes uses to describe the orienting identity of the Proud Boys, "Western chauvinism," suggests

Joey Gibson of Patriot Prayer at "free speech" rally at Evergreen State College, June 15, 2017. Photograph by Jason Wilson.

the link between racism and patriarchy. Along with the endorsement of "traditional" gender roles and male supremacy, the Proud Boys are animated by anti-immigrant restrictionism and hostility to Islam.

McInnes has taken pains to distance himself and his group from white supremacists. He has rejected open racists from the Proud Boys and denounced them on his radio show. He publicly discouraged Proud Boys from attending the Unite the Right rally in Charlottesville, and subsequently blamed the organizers of the rally for Heather Heyer's death. Writing in *Proud Boy Magazine* after Charlottesville, McInnes stated flatly that alt-rightists cannot be Proud Boys: "The two big differences we have with them is the 'JQ' [Jewish Question] and racial identity politics. They think the Jews are responsible for America's problems, and they think 'Western' is inseparable from 'white.' They don't see a future for non-whites in America. FUCK THAT. . . . We openly encourage Jewish and non-white members and want them to know they're at home with us. There are NO racial requirements to be in the Proud Boys.

There are no special rules for black Proud Boys (this overrides anything previously published about black PBs) or any other non-white PBs."[33]

In fact, the Proud Boys ritualistically engage in racial borrowing. *Uhuru*, the Swahili word for "freedom" and a term associated with African liberation struggles, is ubiquitous in Proud Boy, culture—on their Facebook page, on T-shirts, and as a tag line on McInnes's show, always uttered as an affirmation. Perhaps meant ironically, it is nevertheless omnipresent in their culture. Yet there is plenty of connective tissue between McInnes, the Proud Boys, and racist organizations, including views on immigration and against Islam shared with other openly racist groups, and racist statements made over time by McInnes himself.

Watchdog organizations such as the Southern Poverty Law Center have worked to expose McInnes and the Proud Boys as racists hiding behind more neutral language. But what do such exposures actually tell us? Is a clear line crossed when a group or its figurehead makes explicitly racist statements as opposed to anti-Islamic or anti-immigration statements? Indeed, is there any legacy of far-right politics in the United States that has not ultimately been fastened to white supremacy? Would anyone likely to join the Proud Boys, a group that champions "the West" and makes attacking antifascists its most prized activity, not be aware of its adjacency to racist groups and ideas?

One good example of this dynamic juxtaposition of racism and antiracism is captured in a photograph of counter-demonstrating Proud Boys at a "March for Our Lives" gun-control protest in Orlando just after the school shooting in Parkland, Florida, in March 2018. The Proud Boys carry a banner depicting a photograph of captured Apache leader Geronimo and fellow warriors wielding rifles with the caption "TURN IN YOUR ARMS. THE STATE WILL PROTECT YOU." The banner is meant to persuade U.S. citizens to oppose gun-control laws by encouraging an identification with Native Americans forced to surrender to the U.S. state. The equation between gun control for U.S. citizens and the destruction of Apache sovereignty only makes sense at the level of bare affect. But the statement is rendered even more paradoxical in the photograph as the Proud Boy on the left makes a "white power" gesture for the camera. Again, we argue that the important question is not whether a group like the Proud Boys is multiracial, as McInnes claims, or is a racist organization in sheep's clothing, for it is both. The question, then, is *how* symbols of Blackness and multiculturalism ultimately bolster white supremacy.

The Alt-Right, the Alt-Lite, and the Space of Multiculturalism

Openly racist critics of McInnes have seen the Proud Boys as essentially a stopover on the way to white nationalism. As Mike "Enoch" Peinovich, white-nationalist blogger, founder of The Right Stuff, and co-host of the podcast *Daily Shoah* put it: "Let's break down the Proud Boy constituency. . . . If you're a white guy with a white girlfriend or no girlfriend . . . you're just a hair's breath away from jumping into the Alt-Right and just being one of us—being a white nationalist. The other people have certain hang-ups, and it's

Proud Boys at the "March for Our Lives" gun-control rally on March 28, 2018, in Orlando following school shooting in Parkland, Florida. Man on left gives "white power" sign. Photograph by Sam Schaffer.

personal issues. . . . It's that they're Jewish. They're half-white. They're mixed race or they have a non-white girlfriend or wife. . . . So, at the end of the day, and I predict that a year from now Proud Boys are going to be Jews, off-whites, and race-mixers."[34]

As an explicit white nationalist, Peinovich can tolerate mixed-race far-right groups only insofar as they function as a gateway to his vision of a pure white racial state. As Hunter Wallace, a white nationalist writer, similarly noted, the "average 'normie' is more receptive to hearing these messages from Milo Yiannopoulos than from [American Renaissance editor] Jared Taylor, much less from @Pepe_Stormtrooper1488."[35]

The alt-lite might act as a gateway drug for some people who eventually crave the more intense rush of uncut white supremacy advertised by the alt-right. But we argue that it is the liminal space in which white supremacy and multiculturalism interact that generates meaning and power for the far right. As we have argued, U.S. politics has always simultaneously toggled between deep fantasies of racial hierarchy and stated commitments to universal ideals in a mutually supporting dynamic. Movement between these positions has always given cultural meaning and material benefits to whites even as it allows for hegemonic legitimacy in a multiracial society. On the contemporary far right, the potency of white supremacy fuels authoritarian, masculinist notions of national identity for a broader group.

In the coming years, right-wing nationalism is likely to grow in the United States. Massive economic disparity and increasing demographic change are contributing factors, and each makes multiculturalism critical to its growth in distinct ways. The Republican Party has continued a trajectory toward the racist right in terms of its commitment to nativism, anti-Islamism, voter suppression, and "law and order." But the growth of the far right also takes place independently through everything from internet message boards to policy institutes, from street protest to organization building, from small acts of violence to large acts of terror. Its anchored commitments are to "Western civilization," the white race, and patriarchal rule. Such a nationalism will continue to target and demonize certain groups—Muslims, undocumented immigrants, Black protesters, and leftist activists, among others. The main currents of racism in the United States have always been nurtured by a vision of the American nation as already white-dominated.

Samuel Francis, former *Washington Times* editor and columnist, campaign adviser to Pat Buchanan, and intellectual ur-father of the contemporary U.S. far right, put it this way in 1995: "Most white Americans retain too much sense of nationality and too much allegiance to their country and their own communities to accept the proposal of giving up large parts of the US to others (racially different or not). . . . By embracing a strategy that involved breaking up the United States, not only would whites be giving up their own country but also they would be forced to give up appeals to its history, its traditions, and its interests as a nation. . . . [I]n short, we would have to start all over in the project of constructing a culture, a country and a political order."[36]

Francis calls for white racial dominance, but within the confines of the present U.S. state. Such a project requires an embrace of a national identity that unavoidably includes racial difference. And clearly such a vision is built from ambivalent materials in regard to race, from the text of the Constitution to the words of Lincoln, from geographical space shared with increasingly non-white others to the conquest that produced that space. Indeed, one can use both the text of the Constitution and the words of Lincoln to either authorize antiracist universalism or to demonstrate that the United States has been chiefly a racist enterprise historically. But whereas European ethnonationalists like the National Rally in France, the Hungarian Jobbik party, or the Swedish Democrats can—for the time being—indulge national fantasies of white racial purity, the United States is, as a nation, inescapably multiracial from the beginning.

Thus as it continues to vie for hegemony, this right will require selective incorporation. Like longtime racist, paleoconservative commentator, and presidential candidate Patrick Buchanan's choice of African American schoolteacher Ezola Foster as his running mate in his independent run for president in 2000, white American dreams and racial inclusion exist in an uneasy but necessary tension for far-right nationalists. Diehard white supremacists will of course continue to reject multiculturalism, but they exist in a larger ecosystem of the far right. Ethnonationalists such as Richard Spencer, Identity Evropa's Nathan Damigo, and various other white-nationalist groups insist that a separate racial state is necessary to preserve the white race. But this will likely remain a minority position within the populist far right even as it orients the larger movement through anti-immigrant, anti-Muslim, and anti-Black discourse and organization. In some cases, it will continue to require both the symbolic uses of and concrete recruitment of people of color, and at the very least accept the demographic reality of the United States as a multiracial state.

In April 2018, Federal Elections Commission reports revealed that a Wisconsin congressional candidate named Paul Nehlen with ties to white-supremacist groups had paid more than $7,000 to Diamond and Silk to produce an online ad in support of Nehlen's 2016 primary challenge for Paul Ryan's congressional seat. In the ad, Diamond blasts "a.k.a. Lyin' Ryan" for "crippling the American people and the middle class by shipping our jobs overseas. Jobs like GM, Chrysler, and Oscar Mayer wiener," as Silk waves a hot dog at the camera and asks, "What? Oscar?"[37] Nehlen, who later would be described by the *Daily Beast* as "the most prominent white nationalist in U.S. politics," was banned by Facebook in 2018 for his racist and anti-Semitic postings and also disavowed by both the Wisconsin Republican Party and senior editors at Breitbart News.

For Diamond and Silk, the decision to record a video for a candidate who espoused white-supremacist views likely represented a straightforward financial transaction—what they explained in another context as "monetizing their platform."[38] But more important for our analysis is Nehlen's interest in seeking the endorsement of two Black women for a campaign located so unapologetically on the far right. On Nehlen's Facebook page, he posted the video with a comment: "Diamond and Silk are simply the best!" The hundreds of posts from his followers about the video were overwhelmingly enthusiastic—many dozens of recitations of "Love these ladies!"

Video still from Diamond and Silk online campaign ad for Paul Nehlen, 2016 candidate for Wisconsin's First Congressional District.

That supporters of a racist candidate on the far right would rave about the endorsement of two Black women exemplifies the complicated labor of race in the current conjuncture. In the context of the history traced within the last two chapters, even these most unlikely invocations of race should not seem surprising. For a candidate who wishes to position himself as the ethical representative of the abandoned American worker angry at the political establishment's betrayals and infidelities, the invocation of Diamond and Silk makes perfect sense. Just as John McCain's "Joe the Plumber" invoked the hardworking producerist subject in 2008 through his whiteness, Diamond and Silk perform an anti-elitism and irreverence toward established authority through their Blackness. Such incorporations of multiculturalism on the far right will likely increase in the future, and grow in their sophistication and effectiveness.

5
STATE ABANDONMENT AND MILITIA REVOLT
White Occupation, Native Land, and Black Lives

• • •

"Hands Up . . . Don't Shoot!" "Hands Up . . . Don't Shoot!" The call and response echoed across a tense crowd of a few hundred people gathered on a cold Saturday in January. The gathering crowd raised their arms above their heads in surrender, repeating the ubiquitous pose struck by Black Lives Matter protesters across the country in the wake of the 2015 killing of Michael Brown by police in Ferguson, Missouri. Like many of the demonstrations connected to the Movement for Black Lives, this gathering unfolded amid deep economic crisis; unemployment in the surrounding region stood at nearly 20 percent, and the main industries that had once supported life and possibility a generation ago were long in decline. And also, like the Black Lives Matter actions, the protest was organized in the aftermath of a civilian shooting by police and in opposition to a lengthy prison sentence recently handed down to two local residents because of federal mandatory minimum sentencing guidelines.[1]

This protest, however, did not unfold in Chicago, St. Louis, or New York, but in a town of less than two thousand people in sparsely populated eastern Oregon, 125 miles from the Idaho border. The participants were almost entirely white. They were gathered in front of the Harney County Courthouse in Burns, Oregon, in early February 2016 to protest the killing of LaVoy Finicum at the hands of state police. Finicum, an Arizona rancher, had played a central role in the occupation of the nearby Malheur National Wildlife Refuge the month before. The protest, led by an Arizona-based activist named Ammon Bundy, centered nominally on the federal sentences recently given to local ranchers Dwight Hammond Jr. and his son Steven for setting fires (in an effort to control weeds) on their cattle ranch that spread to neighboring federal land. Bundy and the other occupiers framed the occupation as a confrontation with federal authorities over control of rural land and resources, and the occupation soon drew right-wing activists from militia and patriot groups from across the western United States. Finicum was a part of a group that had left the occupation at the refuge to meet with local supporters when their convoy was stopped by police, resulting in a confrontation and shoot-out. A week later, another group of Finicum supporters would organize a "Rural Lives Matter" protest in the town of Halfway, Oregon (population two hundred) to "learn how America was to be governed by principled local government—NOT FEDERAL OVERREACH."[2]

We anchor this chapter in the story of the Malheur National Wildlife Refuge takeover and its broader political and economic contexts and resonances to consider the relationship between the crises unfolding in largely white areas like rural Oregon and those shaping life in predominantly Black communities, such as Ferguson, Missouri, that have given rise to quite different forms of political mobilization. In what ways do the underlying conditions that shape both of these formations converge, even as their social and political visions differ so dramatically? More specifically, what might the protesters in Oregon learn from their counterparts in Ferguson and elsewhere if they are to address their own conditions of precarity? How might a different modality of racial transposition take place here that could draw from the long-standing political insights, strategies, and analyses forged in the crucibles of antiracist struggles?

As we explain, unmistakable currents of deeply gendered white-settler violence and appropriation were apparent throughout the

"Rural Lives Matter" protest in Halfway, Oregon, on February 2, 2016. The picket sign shows Malheur National Wildlife Refuge occupier LaVoy Finicum, who was killed by police in a confrontation several days earlier. Photograph by Jess Campbell.

forty-day occupation of the Malheur National Wildlife Refuge. The occupation's leadership and core supporters articulate a revanchist white producerism: an effort to regenerate social, political, and economic life through a re-creation of settler occupation and violence. But we need not presume that the self-styled militia groups that orchestrated the occupation stand in for all possible forms of political identification and social vision for rural Oregonians who are white. The labor of race here is complicated and contradictory. The "Hands Up . . . Don't Shoot" chant and "All Lives Matter" invocation can be accurately understood as a crass appropriation of a central signifier to Black Lives Matter, an appropriation that erases the very particular ways that state violence targets Black life. In the context of the protests in Ferguson and Baltimore, this form of rhetorical hijacking often uses the "All Lives Matter" (or in other cases "Blue Lives Matter") chant to portray Black Lives Matter protesters as parochial and anti-democratic, their interests antithetical to the greater good. These invocations also obscure the very specific Black feminist critique developed by the three originators of the Black Lives Matter hashtag—Alicia Garza, Patrice Kahn-Cullers, and Opal Tometi—in the aftermath of the murder of Trayvon Martin in 2012.[3]

At the same time, if we draw our focus beyond the occupation's leadership and consider the broader context of state abandonment and the impact of neoliberal restructuring on rural communities, we might see some articulations between the crisis in eastern Oregon and the campaigns against state violence invoked by the "Hands Up . . . Don't Shoot" cries.[4]

Robin Kelley has framed this contradiction in similar terms in considering the deployment of the cry that "All Lives Matter" in the context of extensive state violence against Black communities. "'All Lives Matter' is heard and felt as a belittling or decentering of anti-Black racism," he writes. "It trades on postracial myths of equivalency in suffering. On the other hand, sometimes we react to 'All Lives Matter' with such hostility that it stands in as an unambiguous expression of anti-Black racism. Can we salvage these words? Don't we want to build a world in which every life is valuable, cherished and sustained? Are we not seeking a world that recognizes multiple sites of dispossession and recognizes that state violence inside US borders is inseparable from US militarism around the world?"[5]

The economic and political crisis in rural Oregon seems to constitute a "site of dispossession" for multiple groups: the Native communities whose lands, resources, and sovereignty are subject to constant attack and appropriation; workers from the Global South, particularly rural Mexico, whose labor has been central to many industries in the state, including agriculture, food processing, and forestry; and white-majority communities facing growing economic insecurity, unemployment, and state abandonment. Following Kelley, we should not assume any equivalency of suffering or loss between such groups. The descendants of the settlers do not occupy the same position as the descendants of the indigenous groups who were dispossessed of land and life. But possibilities for political identification and shared action do not stem only from equivalent circumstances or statuses. They come also from shared aspirations and desires, and from a common understanding of relations of power that foreclose life.

The Malheur Occupation

The occupation of the Malheur National Wildlife Refuge in early 2016, headed by Ammon Bundy, must be understood through the commitments and histories of a highly masculinized white-producerist and settler-colonial worldview. The Bundy family, led by Ammon's father, Cliven, had for decades battled with the federal Bureau of Land Management over modest fees Cliven was required to pay in order to graze his cattle on public lands, culminating in an armed standoff at their Nevada ranch in 2014. Right-wing militia activists flocked to the Bundy family's property during that confrontation, relishing the opportunity to stare down federal officials in the name of local authority and property rights. During the Obama presidency in particular, right-wing formations contrasted their producerist ethics to the immoral excesses of the redistributive state. Addressing supporters at his ranch during that standoff, Cliven made these connections clear: "I want to tell you one more thing I know about the Negro. . . . They abort their young children, they put their young men in jail, because they never learned how to pick cotton. And I've often wondered, are they better off as slaves, picking cotton and having a family life and doing things, or are they better off under government subsidy? They didn't get no more freedom. They got less freedom."[6]

While many of Cliven Bundy's high-profile supporters, including Kentucky senator Rand Paul, condemned those comments, Bundy's remarks were inextricably tied to a racialized producerist worldview that has long required anti-Black demonization and the ongoing erasure of Native peoples. The Bundy family, which traces its ranching ties in Nevada to the 1870s, imagine and describe themselves as the sole claimants to the land, a possession they must continually defend from unwarranted federal arrogation. Here, centuries-long conditions of national expansion, imperial violence, and settler conquest must be disavowed in order to conjure and venerate an autonomous and self-determined subject who makes his living, following Locke, by mixing his labor with the land. This mythology, and the forgetting it requires, continues to permeate discourses of "property rights" in the western United States and places profound constraints on the capacity of many people—Native and non-Native alike—to realize any viable responses to the conditions of precarity they now face.

Indeed, the same political histories of white producerism and settler colonialism in the conflict on the Bundy ranch shaped the contours of the Malheur occupation and foreclosed far more oppositional and transformational possibilities. Ammon Bundy's entry point into eastern Oregon in late 2015 was the pending federal sentencing of Dwight and Steven Hammond. The conviction required the Hammonds to be sentenced under the mandatory minimum guidelines of the Antiterrorism and Effective Death Penalty Act of 1996. The judge, however, initially ruled that the required five-year sentences would be too punitive, rejecting the prosecutor's contention that arson on federal land constituted an act of domestic terrorism. But federal prosecutors persisted, and another judge eventually issued a new sentence that adhered to the five-year mandatory minimum.[7]

Although the Hammonds had an uneven reputation in the surrounding community for their repeated clashes with the Bureau of Land Management, the length of the new sentences galvanized many supporters to their side, from organized groups including the Oregon Farm Bureau and the ranchers association to hundreds of the Hammonds' neighbors in eastern Oregon. This was the opening that Ammon Bundy and his followers exploited. Bundy and a small number of supporters relocated to the Burns area in early December 2015, hoping to align the Hammonds, the local residents, and even the Harney County sheriff in a confrontation against federal authorities, hoping that the Hammonds might be granted a kind of sanctuary or asylum by local law enforcement. Such a demand captured the main commitments of the broader "sovereign citizen" movement, a loosely organized network of local activists and organizations who largely reject the authority of federal law. Related groups like the far-right Constitutional Sheriffs and Peace Officers Association, which has counted at least six elected Oregon County sheriffs as members and contends that its sheriffs serve as "the last line of defense standing between the overreaching government and your Constitutionally guaranteed rights."[8] This vision of a brave but besieged white populace declaring its independence from a corrupt state has direct ties to racist formations like Posse Comitatus that were active in the region in the 1980s and 1990s.[9]

Other self-styled militia and patriot groups began descending on Burns as well, answering Ammon Bundy's call to defend the Hammonds from an unlawful federal prosecution. In a video message to supporters the week before the occupation began, a solemn Bundy linked the unjust prosecution and criminal sentences facing the Hammonds to the larger economic crisis besieging the region, arguing that both were tied to the federal government's usurpation of control over land and resources.[10] The rallies organized by the Bundys and their supporters, devoted to "taking back America county by county," linked a suffering populace— "Rural Lives Matter"—to the alleged encroachment by the federal government on "principled local government."

On January 3, 2016, after joining a march of hundreds of local Hammonds supporters in their hometown of Burns, Ammon Bundy broke off with a group of roughly two dozen armed protesters to occupy the Malheur National Wildlife Refuge twenty-six miles away, thus initiating a forty-day standoff. Few local residents joined the occupiers, and many, including the Hammonds, rejected their protest altogether. The refuge itself, managed by the U.S. Fish and Wildlife Service, had no connection to the Hammonds'

"Rural Lives Matter"
Take America Back County by County

RALLY

Sat, February 6th, 2016
HALFWAY, OREGON
Noon – 5pm

DEDICATED TO THE HAMMONDS and TO THE MEMORY OF
LAVOY FINCIUM and JACK YANTIS

- 12:00 pm: START at Halfway Lions Club 235 Lions Street
- Peaceful Protest Main Street March (beginning and ending at Lions Club)
- Speeches & Instruction: Learn how America was to be governed by principled local government – NOT FEDERAL OVERREACH.
- Step by Step process for getting Constitutional County Commissioners and Sheriff that stands for We the People of your county
- Coffee – Soup – Conversation – Discussion at Lions Club
- Come a day early if you want – RV spots available

In Support of Bill of Rights and LOCAL Constitutional
Government
Bring Flags, Signs, Posters

Flyer for "Rural Lives Matter" rally in Halfway, Oregon, on February 6, 2016.

case, the Bureau of Land Management, or the constellation of forces aligned with the Antiterrorism and Effective Death Penalty Act under which they were sentenced. Indeed, the decision to occupy a public bird sanctuary as a response to a draconian criminal sentencing decision and the broader climate of economic decline facing Harney County reveals a great deal about the constraints of the white-producerist politics championed by Bundy and his allies.

The seizure of the refuge was meant to symbolize and unleash a heroic stand against the chief adversary of the occupiers: an oppressive state alleged to have abandoned its subordination to the populace. In this narrative, the armed white men who led the takeover were singularly possessed with the bravery, determination, and insight needed to bring the state to its knees and free the virtuous populace from its command.[11] But from another perspective, the protesters at the refuge in particular and the Hammonds and their supporters in general were latecomers to the struggle against the harsh sentencing practices that would send the father-and-son duo away for so long. The kind of mandatory minimums under which the Hammonds were sentenced had long wreaked havoc on Black and brown communities since they were first adopted in the 1970s in the name of fighting drug abuse and street crime. Since the early 1990s, Oregon voters had also approved a series of ballot measures mandating higher minimum sentences for a wide variety of criminal offenses, effectively doubling the state's prison population in the subsequent fifteen years. What the Hammonds faced in 2015 had been happening to millions of people across the country over the past forty years and to many thousands of people in the state.[12]

Indeed, it was the same predatory and aggressive criminal justice practices—also culminating in a civilian shooting by police—that spurred the large-scale protests in Ferguson, Missouri, in particular and within the Movement for Black Lives in general. Black political organizers had long recognized that an unrelenting system of mass incarceration could not and would not distinguish between the type and seriousness of offenses as it reproduced and expanded its reach and authority. This is not to argue that policing practices in Burns or elsewhere in Oregon resembled the militaristic and intensive forms of policing that Black residents in Ferguson had long endured. They did not. But to point out a relationship here does not require one to insist upon an equivalence. Instead, we argue that social movements in many other parts of the country had noted for decades what the Bundys had only recently discovered. Organizers of the Movement for Black Lives had already rendered a sophisticated and prescient analysis of the bellicose modes of surveillance, militarization, and warehousing that characterized the twenty-first-century criminal justice system.[13] While their framework focused on the impacts of this system on Black communities and Black life, and its imbrication with a long history of anti-Black racism, the Hammonds case in particular and the rise of mass incarceration in the predominantly white state of Oregon in general has demonstrated that whiteness provides an uneven protection from the same state violence. Indeed, there were organizations in Oregon, including the statewide Partnership for Safety and Justice, that had been foregrounding these connections for many years and advocating for precisely the kind of reforms that would have restricted the sentencing practices that ensnared the Hammonds. Yet the white-producerist vision, which is deeply invested in a sovereign subject heroically reclaiming his autonomy, is incapable of tracing such connections and interdependences. Rather than seek out allies or investigate the history and structure of such practices, they took over a birding site with assault rifles.[14]

In the midst of the Malheur occupation, many commentators observed that the popular outrage in response to the Hammonds' sentence could not be separated from the larger economic decline and crisis facing the region. As Bundy emphasized in his video message to supporters, in the early 1970s, Harney County had boasted the highest per capita income in Oregon. Forty years later, the county, a vast expanse of high desert twice as large as Connecticut but with a population of only eight thousand, had one of the highest unemployment rates in the state (it approached 17 percent during the recession in 2009). Nearly two-thirds of the county's children qualify for free or reduced-price lunch.[15] From

Bundy's perspective, the occupation was also meant to protest and indict the role of the federal government in denying the people of Harney County their way of life and access to "their land and resources."

What Bundy's account omitted was that the collapse of the local economy, centered in large part on the closing of several timber mills in the area, was tied to the broader decline of the timber industry in the Pacific Northwest. While many blame environmental regulations and increased government oversight for the decline in timber production, the historian Steven Beda has shown that these forces did not play a decisive role in the industry's decline. Beda demonstrates that a much broader constellation of events and conditions, including shifts in global timber markets, the short-term-profit imperatives of companies that purchased tracts of timber-rich lands, and the uneven patterns of economic and political development between urban and rural areas across the Northwest, played a much larger role.[16] While formidable unions like the International Woodworkers of America had once given labor a potent voice in the industry, their gradual decline in the mid-twentieth century left timber workers increasingly defenseless against these forces. Easing environmental regulations would do little to restore the jobs and economic activity generated by timber production a generation ago. Indeed, Harney County's economic crisis had resulted not from the public ownership of forestlands but from private ownership and control, along with the market forces within which all private ownership must operate. Chuck Willer of the Coast Range Association describes these contemporary conditions as "Wall Street forestry" because of the high concentration of corporate holdings of forestry lands in Oregon through real estate investment trusts that are taxed at lower levels. Willer concludes that the lower tax rates paid by these holding companies, secured in part through a broader lowering of property-tax rates in the mid-1990s supported by the timber industry, reduced revenues to rural counties already in the throes of fiscal crisis.[17] Transferring the land from public to private ownership, as the Bundys and many of their supporters demanded, would not address these dynamics.

Also missing in Ammon Bundy's account was any mention of the employment sector that was almost singularly responsible for protecting Harney County from a much deeper crisis: public-sector employment. Some 45 percent of jobs in the county are with state and local government—the largest share in all of Oregon. Moreover, federal public employment has remained relatively stable even as private-sector employment has continued to decline since the Great Recession. These patterns hold true for almost all of the timber-dependent counties in eastern and southern Oregon; the same government that is the object of the occupiers' resentment is one of the only bulwarks providing some protection from the ravages of the market.[18] It has primarily been cuts to state and local government, fueled by property-tax limitations and job losses, that have hurt rural economies.[19]

If the Bundys and the other occupiers wanted to have a discussion about the federal government's role in appropriating and

Malheur National Wildlife Refuge occupiers Ammon and Ryan Bundy asking Harney County farmers and ranchers in Crane, Oregon, to destroy their grazing agreements with the federal government, January 18, 2016. Photograph by Peter Walker.

managing lands, and the dispossessions that can ensue, they could have bypassed the wildlife refuge and headed to the aging trailers housing the offices of the nearby Burns Paiute Tribe, located just thirty miles from the refuge's visitor center. The Malheur refuge itself is located on the ancestral lands of the Paiute Tribe. Following the 1878 Bannock War, the Paiute people were forcibly removed by the federal government, which seized 1.5 million acres of ancestral homelands from the tribe. Nearly a third of that land is now under private ownership. In the late 1960s, after a decades-long legal battle, individual tribal members received checks for $743.20 as compensation. The tribe eventually won back a sliver of the land (about 760 acres) that today constitutes the Burns Paiute reservation.

When Ammon Bundy insisted during the standoff that "the land titles need to be transferred back to the people," he was recapitulating the long process of settler dispossession and disavowal, a dynamic that Burns Paiute leaders were quick to challenge. Tribal chair Charlotte Rodrique explained at a press conference shortly after the occupation began that "this is still our land no matter who's living on it." The tribal leadership also noted the glaring disparities in the ways the state responded to the Malheur refuge takeover and the long history of violence that has faced Native people in the region. Tribal council member Jarvis Kennedy asked, "I wonder if it was a bunch of natives that went out there and overtook that, or any federal land, would they let us come into town and get supplies and re-up?" He noted, "They didn't ask anybody, we don't want them here."[20]

Tribal governments in the Northwest have a long history of advocacy to "decolonize the land," thinking in sophisticated ways about how to balance economic activity, ecological sustenance and restoration, and tribal sovereignty (including traditional tribal land-use practices) under conditions of large-scale federal land ownership. Groups like the Burns Paiute Natural Resources Department hold much of this knowledge, analysis, and capacity.[21] In addition, as geographer Peter Walker points out in his ethnographic account of the occupation, much of the local resistance to the Bundy-led takeover was made possible because of a long history of collaboration between local communities and public agencies around these same questions.[22] But the producerist framework championed by the occupiers could not countenance or imagine such relationships of reciprocity. They were not dependent on anyone.

Producerist Rage and Neoliberal Abandonment

While the occupation of the Malheur Refuge was a violent and extreme confrontation with federal authorities over questions of property ownership and state violence, the action was in many ways quite consistent with a dominant political vision rooted in white-settler producerism that continues to shape political identifications in the region today. For example, in Oregon's Josephine County, another sprawling expanse of forestland in the southwestern corner of the state facing a major economic crisis, a militia group initiated a similar confrontation with federal authorities. As in many timber-dependent economies in the state, for much of the twentieth century, a portion of revenues of timber harvests funded public services in Josephine County. In 1975 the county had twenty-two timber mills. The last closed in 2013.[23] For a time the federal government made up for the losses by providing payments directly to counties affected by declines in timber revenue in order to pay for schools and basic services, particularly public safety. That funding steadily declined during the last ten years, from $14 million in 2007–8 to less than $2 million by 2014–15. The same trends have taken place in every timber-dependent county in Oregon. Large rural counties with sparse populations, high levels of unemployment and underemployment, and a diminished tax base cannot meet basic funding needs, especially for public safety. In the early 1990s, Oregon voters passed a series of ballot measures to amend the state constitution to severely limit local property-tax rates. Josephine County voters, like many others in the state, have rejected more than a dozen tax measures to raise property taxes in order to pay for basic services.[24]

As a result, 911 service across much of the county is spotty at best. In 2013, years of budget cuts left the Josephine County

Sheriff's Office with a single deputy to respond to general calls across the entire county; a few years earlier there had been twenty-two. Patrol service takes place for only eight hours a day, five days a week, and it is only during those times that the sheriff's office can respond to life-threatening emergencies. In 2012 the sheriff's office offered residents the grim advice that "if you know you are in a potentially volatile situation (for example, you are a protected person in a restraining order that you believe the respondent may violate), you may want to consider relocating to an area with adequate law enforcement services."[25]

The sheriff's office closed its major crimes unit. The records division was also closed; residents who wish to report crimes can go online and log the information themselves, but only for the purposes of record keeping. No investigation or response will follow. As reported burglaries and theft cases increased by more than 70 percent, applications in the county for concealed handguns rose 50 percent. In early 2013 the *Grants Pass Daily Courier* reported that a laid-off deputy was organizing an armed citizen group in order to respond to burglaries and other crimes; several armed civilian patrols began operating that year across the county, in addition to a citizen task force that the sheriff's office has trained to investigate crimes.[26]

In May 2007, all four public libraries in Josephine County were closed due to lack of funding. They eventually reopened as privately run public libraries, relying primarily on a volunteer staff and contributions from members. Since then several mental health and transportation programs have been privatized or eliminated. A youth shelter and counseling center also closed.[27]

Grover Norquist famously explained, "I don't want to abolish government. I simply want to reduce it to the size where I can drag it into the bathroom and drown it in the bathtub."[28] As much as anywhere in the country, in Josephine County the local state at least thrashes about in the tub, appearing to gasp its last. The only revenue source keeping the sheriff's office open now is the federal government.

In April 2015, when the Bureau of Land Management questioned a claim by a miner at the Sugar Pine Mine, leaders of a local militia group, the Josephine County Oath Keepers, raced into action. They framed the bureau's actions as a constitutional abrogation, insisting that the agency was preparing to burn the miners' equipment without a hearing, a charge the agency repeatedly denied. The local bureau office had to be temporarily closed because of mounting death threats; like elsewhere in the West, federal employees in routine jobs began to fear for their lives.

The Josephine County Oath Keepers chapter was started in 2013 by a former national guardsman and aviator named Joseph Rice, and it seeks to distance itself from the white nationalist militia formations of the 1990s. As one member told a reporter from *Vice* magazine, "We're not toothless rednecks. We don't do the Aryan shit—that's the complete opposite of what we want. That's not freedom. That's not equality. We've done classes on everything from small-animal butchering to sewing. We're just out to help each other out, help *people* out." Indeed, a significant portion of the group's ongoing work attempts to respond to vulnerabilities produced by state abandonment, using such projects to cultivate an anti-statist politics. The group runs regular emergency preparedness trainings for members and volunteers, has formed a sophisticated short-wave radio communications network to reach deep into rural regions of the county, has organized members to build wheelchair ramps at homes, and has organized repairs at the local county fairgrounds and a local elementary school.[29] In other communities such "community service" activities have little political significance; in Josephine County they are meant to serve also as a critique of state dependence and to invoke a vision of frontier autonomy and self-determination. Many people in eastern and southern Oregon who are not members of these militias nonetheless have expressed sympathy for movement aims, or express anger toward what they see as arrogant federal bureaucrats who have undue influence over their lives.

Here, then, is the great paradox of state abandonment for rural Oregon in a moment of deep economic crisis. As rural counties and communities become ever more dependent on the federal and state governments redistributing income their way, organized antigovernment currents only sharpen and multiply. The extraction economies that shaped the legacy of these regions no longer require the labor of those living there, and the government does little to address their precarious situation. Meanwhile, real estate values and many employment sectors in the Portland metropolitan area prosper. The depth and impact of the economic shifts and governmental neglect in places like Josephine County is unprecedented. To read the rise of paramilitary activity at this moment as solely an expression of white nationalism risks missing the ways that changing political and economic conditions during the last thirty years have provided such fertile ground for paramilitary and other patriot movement organizing.

Again, these conditions are long familiar to aggrieved Black and brown populations in rural and urban areas alike. The conditions of unemployment, crisis, and abandonment that have come to Josephine County in the last thirty years have been well known to the people of Ferguson, Baltimore, and Flint for more than a generation. And in those places, popular efforts to redress those conditions have turned to demands on the state as well as private actors. In Ferguson, for example, protesters linked the rise in police violence and the precarity and crisis that gripped the city to the ways that large corporations, such as locally based Emerson Electronics, continue to extract public subsidies for private enrichment, offering few economic benefits to the surrounding community. Demands from Black community and labor organizations in Ferguson and elsewhere insist that the state has a responsibility to address these conditions by helping to generate living wage jobs, fund public services, and address police violence. The broad platform of the national Movement for Black Lives addresses the specificity of anti-Black racism and state violence, but it also presses wide-ranging demands for the right of workers to organize, increased regulations over banks and large-scale financial institutions, large-scale investment in public-employment projects, robust environmental protections, and an explicit call to address economic predation and inequality.[30] These policies, if realized, would do far more to ensure that "All Lives Matter" in rural Oregon than any demand advanced by those who seized a bird refuge.

Yet in the predominantly white communities of rural Oregon beset by many of the same problems, the Bundys, militia groups, and other forces speaking in producerist tones advance much different demands. Long abandoned by private elites and devastated by market forces, they rage against the very state that supplies the resources that keep their communities economically viable.

So what accounts for the appeal of this anti-statist rage? In a very basic sense, the assertion that the federal government dictates the terms of life for people in white rural communities is a claim about citizens not having control over governance in any meaningful sense. The other side of this perception of political powerlessness is the increasingly obvious reality that this same state does not protect these people, does not buoy them, does not offer the prospect of moving them out of a spiral of economic decline.

Militia groups and their supporters generally disdain the idea of being dependent on the state. Psychoanalyst Melanie Klein offered perhaps the greatest insights about fears of dependence in this way. For her, distress about dependence reflects deeper insecurities about one's own safety and viability if support is withdrawn. "Dependence is felt to be dangerous because it involves the possibility of privation," she writes. It is not difficult to imagine such fear in the context of a state that appears to offer nothing that could help people live sustainable lives—nor provides the opportunity for them to influence state action. In the frontier imaginary, land is a source of freedom insofar as it provides direct livelihood through its exploitation. Seen this way, federal control of land is in direct violation of the liberty of individuals and local communities. Thus we see the call for federal deeds to be voided, private owners to take over federal property, and federal grazing permits to be vacated. An armed takeover of a public bird sanctuary epitomizes these dynamics.

The enemies and threats invoked by the militia movement are not those of white nationalists. The rhetoric used to build their movement in southern and eastern Oregon asserts neither race nor racial animus as a basis of struggle. Yet is there something here that connects anti-statism to both race and empire for the militias? First, the very frontier narrative of autonomy, freedom, and defense of land secured through violence reenacts and is made meaningful through a lens of conquest over and against indigenous inhabitants. Second, the militia organizations active in Oregon—the Three Percenters, Oath Keepers, and patriot organizations—present themselves as formations made up largely of military veterans whose role is to protect against internal and external threats to the nation.[31]

The state in the militia imaginary is thus demonic precisely when it is seen to take land from local individual citizens and communities for its own purposes or when it is seen to cause dependency. The era of the contemporary militia movement began symbolically with 9/11 (an invasion from without) and was continued by the election of a Black Democratic president (an alien threat from within). For the militias, perceived foreign and domestic threats are woven into a singular demonic entity that seeks to destroy the freedom, security, and traditions of western ranchers, miners, and loggers. Racial and gendered fantasies of independence and of a demonic state are co-constituted through a story of rights-bearing individuals endangered by public goods in the form of the Bureau of Land Management and its agents.

The legacies of white supremacy, the frontier, and Lockean beliefs in individual agency act as boundary conditions within which the Malheur occupiers and their militia supporters act. Yet as we see here, the historical specificity of increasing abandonment of a growing number of white people, particularly in marginalized rural areas, complicates the contention that white nationalism alone motivates the political disruptions and formations witnessed in these areas.

The deployment of the "Hands Up . . . Don't Shoot!" cry by Finicum supporters in Harney County following his death exemplifies these contradictions. On the one hand, the appropriation of the chant fails in every way to engage the deep history of Black political organizing, analysis, and struggle that gave rise to these words. In this way, it captures the myopic and often deliberate process of disavowal and repudiation of Black life that continually structures white political identity. On the other hand, the attempt to make visible some feeling of collective suffering and distress through a signifier so closely associated with Black insurgency at least hints at another possibility.

The oppressive state as governing signifier in the militia movement encourages interpretive frames that make militias analogous to contemporary Black protests against police killings. Dismissing the "Hands Up, Don't Shoot" chant or "Rural Lives Matter" meme as merely an attempt to mau-mau those who protest anti-Black violence fails to come to terms with the profound sense of fear and loss animating this movement—and to see that the threat to possessive individualism and perceived liberal sovereignty is itself at such an intense register that it overwhelms racial terms in any direct sense.

The possibilities of identification between Black protest and militia supporters themselves are enhanced by the lived reality that both see state violence as a fundamental issue. When asked about the parallel, Ammon Bundy told CNN that there were "probably similarities" between his movement and Black Lives Matter. This equivalential chain was rendered more concrete when Portland Black Lives Matter joined the militia movement in opposing a Democrat-sponsored bill in the Oregon state legislature written in the wake of LaVoy Finicum's killing that would shield police officers who kill civilians from having their names released.[32]

At the same time, right-wing anti-regulatory and anti-environmentalist interests vie for the allegiance of the denizens of the rural West and the militia movement in particular. In a surprising gesture in July 2018, President Trump signed an official clemency order for the pardon of Dwight and Steven Hammond.[33] The move signaled support for the Malheur takeover from the highest political office in the United States and established a strong link between Trumpism and the militia movement. The person perhaps most responsible for the pardon was an Indiana multimillionaire who made his fortune distributing automotive oil products, Forrest Lucas. A close friend of Vice President Mike Pence, Lucas is also the founder of Protect the Harvest, an organization dedicated to "working to protect your right to hunt, fish, farm, eat meat, and own pets."[34] The nonprofit works to dismantle environmental rules and oppose laws against the mistreatment of livestock through a large and complex lobby with close ties to other members of the Trump administration, including Interior Secretary Ryan Zinke and Agriculture Secretary Sonny Perdue. Lucas's organization marries settler-colonial fantasies of frontier independence to a pro-business deregulatory agenda, as was done in the Sagebrush Rebellion in the 1970s and the "wise use" movement in the 1980s and 1990s. The pardoning of the Hammonds, however, was the first time a president intervened directly by pardoning federal convictions.

The Malheur occupation and the rise of militias more generally in Oregon have demonstrated the contradictory ways in which white political identity becomes mobilized, inhabited, contested, and transformed in the context of crisis and abandonment. As we have argued, the more people in rural Oregon are abandoned by the state, the greater the possibility for anti-statist sentiment to grow. The more people are forced out of the social contract (dwindling resources for schools, infrastructure, etc.), the more they are forced to try to be self-reliant. This path is easier to take than making demands on the state, because such demands are experienced as dangerous dependency—and as a diminution of freedom.

The potential for racialized violence in a climate increasingly shaped by militant anti-statist rhetoric and organization in Oregon should not be underestimated. Oregon has a long history of white violence, exclusion, and land dispossession. At the same time, the depth and impact of neoliberal and state abandonment in places like Josephine County is unprecedented. To read the rise of militia activity at this moment as only an expression of unreconstructed white nationalism risks missing the ways that these conditions provide ground for the development of contradictory forms of white political identity, which may in turn generate new assemblages.

Beyond White Producerism

In this book we have continually returned to the point that white economic decline is not the same as Black and brown economic decline, and that the negative relationship to state power in white communities is not the same as that in Black and brown communities. To stick with our Oregon example for a moment longer: while the residents of Josephine County have lost state support for basic services, the residents of Ferguson are systematically preyed upon by the local state. Rural Oregonians quarrel with a federal Bureau of Land Management that is seen to put clean rivers before the well-being of gold miners, while residents of Flint were left unprotected from water contamination. The Malheur occupiers took over a federal wildlife refuge and held it for six weeks before federal agents began arrests and forced removals. Undocumented members of communities all over the United States are subject to sudden sweeps, arrests, detention, and deportation by federal agents at any time, any place.

In general terms there is a vast economic gap between the richest Americans and everyone else, and the increase in repressive state power and control affects everyone. The intensification of both of these phenomena in the United States in the last half century was made possible to a great extent through a racialized discourse that demonized public provision, wealth redistribution, and regulation, and promoted ever more severe forms of state surveillance, repression, and incarceration. In other words, the increasing economic precarity, vulnerability to state repression, drug and alcohol abuse, emotional distress, and shrinking life expectancy of a growing number of white Americans is causally linked to the racialized legacy of U.S. politics since the 1960s, making them only its most recent victim.

For decades, liberal political commentators have puzzled over why working-class white Americans acted against their economic interests by voting for Republicans. Such was the source of fascination with Democratic pollster Stanley Greenberg's "Reagan Democrats," white union members in the Rust Belt. It is also the question posed by Thomas Frank's 2004 best-seller *What's the Matter with Kansas?* The conceit that economic interests are somehow prior to politics as opposed to being a product of it left such commentators unable to grapple with the many elements at play in political identity—among them racial status, gender, religious faith, and a sense of having political influence on the decisions governing one's life and community. In any case, Frank's question seems almost quaint today, when a majority of whites who voted in the 2016 presidential election chose not merely an economic conservative who is willing to play the race card but an openly racist, authoritarian nationalist.

However, the instability produced by the neoliberal reorganization of the state and the economy opens the door to diverse political possibilities, as evidenced by the Movement for Black Lives, the immigrant rights struggle, Native American resistance, a newly radicalized feminist movement, and LGBTQ militancy. The economic dislocation and growing sense of political powerlessness expressed by white Americans need not gain expression in far-right politics. Indeed, people classified as white have always resisted class rule and state repression and have joined larger movements for freedom. But as W. E. B. Du Bois, James Baldwin, and many others have observed, it is precisely the deeply held investments in whiteness that make it least possible for an emancipatory politics among white Americans.

Expressed politically, whiteness in the United States has linked individualism, autonomy, property, and the work ethic and contrasted them negatively with dependence, poverty, and idleness. This set of contrasts has not merely been assigned to racialized subjects over time. It has produced racial meaning itself. As we have tried to demonstrate in this book, these qualities can be assigned to new racial subjects to stabilize the dominant political and economic order and stave off fundamental political change. Thus political investments in whiteness not only increasingly fail to protect white subjects but also curtail broader visions of freedom expressed as interdependence, care, economic equality, and time spent pleasurably and meaningfully.

CONCLUSION

From Racial Transposition to
New Visions of Political Identity

• • •

On a sunny day in early June 2018, Joey Gibson called out to a crowd of several dozen people gathered for another Patriot Prayer "freedom march" in downtown Portland. Gibson introduced a participant whom he had invited to address the group, a middle-aged Black man who wore a red "Make American Great Again" cap. Gibson announced facetiously, "We got a Black Nazi here! We got a Black Nazi." It was a retort aimed at the hundreds of counter-protesters who had mobilized to oppose the demonstration, some of whom called Gibson and his followers Nazis.

The speaker began: "There's always been a fire in the heart of patriots; people who want to self-govern. They want to be with their own community, in a safe environment, with the rule of law, with no interference from the government, or other political parties." A bystander called out, "Sounds like anarchism!" The speaker responded, "Amen."

The speaker continued: "There's been a march of patriots of every color—black, brown, white, yellow—that have given so much to this country. . . . We're empowered by the Constitution and the freedom of all mankind, no matter where they're from, what they look like, or their beginnings in life." He then pointed to the counter-protesters, standing across the street, many affiliated with the antifascist group Antifa, declaring, "They over there want collectivism, and collectivism is death and lack of freedom. Don't let it happen. We got to fight and stand up forever."[1] The crowd cheered loudly before following another speaker in reciting the Pledge of Allegiance, hands over hearts.[2]

Gibson's "Black Nazi" captures much of the beguiling labor of race in the time of intensifying economic and social inequality addressed in this book. On the one hand, Patriot Prayer and a growing number of like-minded groups share many of the defining characteristics of fascist or protofascist formations. Patriot Prayer venerates masculine honor, hierarchy, authoritarian culture, and a defense of the West.[3] They seek out violent confrontations with groups on the left such as Antifa, and they have also held demonstrations targeting Planned Parenthood. Their rallies draw groups like the "Western chauvinist" Proud Boys and others on the right. The June 3 march attracted several members of the "Hell Shaking Street Preachers," a far-right homophobic group that has protested Portland's LGBT Pride parade; others have drawn unapologetic white supremacists.[4] At a chaotic and often violent Patriot Prayer–led rally in Portland two months later, Tiny Toese and others wore shirts with large block letters saying "Pinochet Did Nothing Wrong" and featuring the letters "RWDS" (Right Wing Death Squad) on the sleeves. (The Chilean dictator, whose death squads terrorized Chile throughout the 1970s and 1980s, is proudly invoked by some on the far right today.)[5]

On the other hand, across these rallies, Patriot Prayer regularly deploys narratives of multiracial incorporation and even antiracism. Gibson continuously and strategically draws on this apparent paradox, referencing people of color within Patriot Prayer as a way to mock critics who describe the group as fascist, as his "Black Nazi" comment made clear. At an August 2017 "freedom of speech" rally in downtown Seattle, as Gibson prepared to introduce Tiny Toese and counter-protesters booed, he asked them mockingly, "You guys don't like Tiny? You don't like men that are brown? You don't like islanders?"[6]

For Gibson, the embrace of a hard-right authoritarianism coexists with support for policies that are beyond the ambit of conventional right-wing politics. As we explained in the Introduction, Gibson described mass incarceration and mandatory minimum sentencing as "legal slavery" that has been "completely disruptive to the Black community." He voiced sympathy for Black Lives Matter and that movement's struggles against police brutality and state violence. Gibson backs the recognition of same-sex marriage and has endorsed a path to citizenship for at least some undocumented immigrants. He told us he "didn't have a fear of Islam" and that "We have to allow communities to do what they want, to stand up for what they want. . . . Right now, I'm more concerned about our government than I am about Islam."[7] The far right, particularly fascists, have always drawn on leftist politics to expand their ranks.[8] But the syncretic intermingling of left and right has often been accomplished by fixing race in place. Today we see signs across the political spectrum that make a conventional political compass seem inadequate.

As we described in chapter 4, Steve Bannon has established himself as a central figure on the populist right who has met with ethnonationalist groups in Europe and regularly airs nativist and Islamophobic sentiments. At the same time, portions of speeches on economic nationalism and community reinvestment he has made to Black business groups can strangely sound like a Black anti-imperialist. Bannon inveighed in one presentation against the "destruction of the Black and Hispanic working class" and asked participants to imagine if the $5.6 trillion that had been spent in "the global war on terror" since 2001 had instead been invested in "Baltimore, in St Louis, and in South Central LA and in Detroit." He charged that the "imperial capital of Wall Street" and both political parties permitted the loss of millions of manufacturing jobs in those cities.[9] When our research led us to attend a large rally for Donald Trump in Oregon during the 2016 Republican primaries, we spoke to several people who told us they had been to a local Bernie Sanders rally the week before and were still deciding which of the two they might support. One large-scale survey has estimated that hundreds of thousands of Sanders supporters (perhaps as many as one in ten) voted for Trump in the general election, a reminder of the instabilities in identification and political formation in play at this moment.[10]

Republican representative Mia Love and Republican senator Tim Scott—supporters of every regressive policy in the contemporary GOP—refer to the need for Black uplift, well-being, and community empowerment to their adoring Tea Party backers. Similarly, Sonnie Johnson, host of *Sonnie's Corner*, a weekly show on Breitbart Radio's conservative "Patriot" station on Sirius XM, explains: "I'm Black. I'm a woman. I was born into a broken home, poverty. I love hip hop." Johnson asserts that the show, which features hip hop interludes between segments, "allows me to mix my conservative intellect with my hip hop culture to bring a renaissance of Black entrepreneurship, economic independence, and political power." A personal friend of the conservative network's late namesake, Andrew Breitbart, Johnson is a frequent guest on Fox News and a speaker at Tea Party and other conservative gatherings. In 2016 Breitbart tapped Johnson to host dozens of local meetups around the country to network with conservative activists in advance of the presidential election.[11] These were not public-relations stunts designed to indemnify conservatives from liberal criticism about their racial intolerance. Johnson, like Kay Coles James and Mia Love, is a conservative movement builder who narrates her ideological commitments through her identity as a Black woman to an overwhelmingly white political base.

We do not review these examples to suggest some kind of softening of the ideological conflicts that constitute the current political landscape. We are indeed in a moment of pitched political struggle, with life-and-death consequences. Nor do these examples suggest that the contemporary right should be regarded as more democratic and egalitarian than previously thought. It should not. Many of the conservative forces that engage and deploy the language of multiculturalism, civil rights, and Black uplift champion policies and worldviews that worsen material and social inequalities; sharpen state violence, militarism, and authoritarian governance; and make greater numbers of people vulnerable to early death.

Yet it would be a mistake to interpret the cases discussed in this book as forms of distraction or mystification that only serve to obscure more authentic relations of power. Victoria Hattam and Joseph Lowndes have demonstrated that political change progresses precisely such through "acts of *recombination*," when seemingly disparate social identities and "ideational fragments" become reorganized into new associative links. Seen this way, "interests and identities are not given in advance" but are instead "made and remade" through shifts in political discourse and identification. This is precisely the work of many figures examined in this book through a process we have described as racial transposition. Thus, efforts to link civil rights norms to right-wing political projects or connect white poverty to a culture of dependence may seem in our moment to be incongruous, but it is precisely in the "words used, the political appeals made, and the identifications evoked" that "otherwise disparate elements are recombined into apparently coherent political positions."[12]

If we presume that the political right today remains unchanged since the era of the Southern Strategy, or if we imagine that the white ethnonationalists who descended on Charlottesville in August 2017 stand in for the entirety of contemporary right-wing politics, we will be unprepared to challenge the growth of these movements in the future. Similarly, if we imagine that whiteness operates as a kind of magic amulet that protects everyone who identifies as white from the ravages of economic predation and state violence, we will narrow the social and political base that might resist such conditions. We can analyze the changing dynamics in right-wing formations, including their fluid deployments of race, while still providing a sober account of the violence and dispossessions they ultimately enact and the hierarchies they protect.

The specific conditions of our current historical moment matter immensely here. Aziz Rana argues that the present conjuncture bears the greatest similarity not to the end of Reconstruction or the Civil War but to the longer Gilded Age. He explains: "In the 1890s, the US suffered the most violent labor conflicts in the world; in the 1930s, developments in the US caused the greatest global capitalist crisis in history. . . . At the same time, unreconstructed white supremacy remained part of the country's drinking water. A majority believed the United States was an intrinsically white republic under extreme duress from recently emancipated, migrating black populations and growing numbers of southern European and Asian immigrants." The period that separates that time from ours is the long Cold War era, which settled labor conflicts through the New Deal and racial conflicts through the civil rights movement, each fostered through U.S. imperial expansion. In the collapse of the New Deal order, the decline of the civil rights movement, and the end of the Cold War, new politics have emerged that are more ideologically diverse, more polarized, and more open to novel articulations.[13]

The cases examined in this book demonstrate the contradictory labor of race in the current moment. Racial meanings have become increasingly flexible, recombinant, and surprising, even as they continue to shore up white supremacy and neoliberal inequality. These instances also stand in sharp contrast to the dominant mode of analysis, which treats contemporary political identifications and interests as fixed and unchanging, determined more by divergent cultural norms and habits than by the complex co-constitutive histories of race and class formation. We now critique examples of this dominant mode in detail, because their implicit assumptions foreclose our capacity to challenge race and class domination both analytically and politically.

The White Precariat as Noble Savage

During Trump's surprising victory in the Republican primaries and subsequent presidential election, countless odes to the misunderstood "white working class" issued forth from the laptops of journalists and scholars. Although treated as revelation, this rediscovery of the long-suffering white America is an episodic ritual that has been performed with every Republican victory since 1968. Following Nixon's victory over Humphrey, *Harpers,* the *New Yorker, Commentary,* and other magazines competed to best capture and describe this group, known variously as "Middle America," "forgotten Americans," or the "Silent Majority." *Time* magazine made "Middle Americans" the Men and Women of the Year in 1970.[14] Regardless of the name, this supposed demographic was described as leading a "backlash" against criminals, demonstrators, and welfare recipients below and liberal elites above. When Ronald Reagan was elected in 1980 there was renewed focus on what Democratic pollster Stanley Greenberg called "Reagan Democrats," union members who were driven by their resentment of the very poor, feminists, the unemployed, African Americans, Latino/as, and other groups. In the 1990s, Democrats, fearing conservative resurgence and influenced by works such as Thomas Edsall and Mary Edsall's *Chain Reaction: The Impact of Race, Rights, and Taxes on American Politics*, explicitly courted what Bill Clinton called "angry white men."[15] Following George W. Bush's election in 2000 came Ruy Teixeira and Joel Rogers's *America's Forgotten Majority: Why the White Working Class Still Matters.*[16]

With the campaign and election of Donald Trump came new versions of this lament about the white working class that got away. But the story has undergone a change. When Reagan ran for president in 1980, non-Hispanic whites made up 88 percent of the electorate; today they are 69 percent and steadily dropping.[17] And as we have discussed in previous chapters, white middle- and working-class fortunes have long been in decline. Thus the current crop of books and articles focused (often interchangeably) on Trump supporters, white southerners, white workers, or the white poor treat them—either positively or negatively—as a distinctly different population. In much the same way that racialized groups have historically been depicted in mirrored doubles as good and bad, noble and threatening, happy and violent, here we can see the depiction of the figure of the "white worker" in either romantic or abjected terms. Whether seen as resentful, self-destructive, and bigoted or as a forgotten figure of lost American pride and virtue, this class is treated increasingly as a projection screen for both the liberal and conservative imagination.

In a widely circulated article just after the 2016 election called "What So Many People Don't Get about the U.S. Working Class," the feminist legal scholar Joan C. Williams made a plea to progressives to bridge the "class culture gap." Confessing her personal socioeconomic distance from this class, she went on to employ the well-worn language of producerism to describe the virtues and resentments of her subjects. Williams soon expanded the popular article into a book titled *White Working Class: Overcoming Class Cluelessness in America*.[18] As is already evident in the title, Williams uses the terms "blue collar," "working class," and "white working class" interchangeably, thereby naturalizing labor as white and foreclosing any possibility of an honest reckoning. She sets out to answer the questions that apparently most rankle a liberal audience still reeling from Trump's election with chapter titles such as "Why Does the Working Class Resent the Poor?" "Why Does the Working Class Resent Professionals But Admire the Rich?" and "Why Don't the People Who Benefit Most from Government Help Seem to Appreciate It?" The white working class, we learn, resents the poor because it values hard work, responsibility, and independence. Its members resent professionals because among other things they value good character and dedication to family over career, acquisitiveness, and social climbing.

This view of a self-contained, singular, and coherent "white working class" finds expression in other highly influential accounts as well. In *Strangers in Their Own Land*, Arlie Hochschild describes the quest that takes the Berkeley-based sociologist into distant Louisiana on an ethnographic "journey into the heart of the right."[19] She explains her motivation for examining her exotic subjects: "If I could truly enter the minds and hearts of people on the far right on the issues of the water they drink, the animals they hunt, the lakes they swim in, the streams they fish in, the air they breathe, I could get to know them up close." Politics and struggles for power, Hochschild concludes, are really rooted in distinct cultural difference. As she puts it, "I came to realize the Tea Party was not so much an official political group as a culture, a way of seeing and feeling about a place and its people." There is no doubt that the white Louisianans with whom Hochschild spoke had strong feelings about their politics, but these feelings are not simply a natural property. The culture she observed is shaped by particular historical conflicts to which Hochschild pays almost no attention.[20] With little notice to histories of political development in Louisiana or the greater South, the race- and class-mediated movements it has produced, or the interests and investments pursued by distinct political actors today, we are only left with a narrative of static cultural particularity which she depicts as conservative America writ small.

The legal scholar and writer Amy Chua offers perhaps the most dismal form of this argument in her 2018 book *Political Tribes*, which suggests that nearly all contemporary political antagonisms can be traced to a preternatural expression of tribal instincts. In a rehash of the social Darwinist William Graham Sumner's late-nineteenth-century concept of "folkways," Chua asserts that a "tribal instinct" to both belong and to exclude explains social, economic, and political conflict across most of world history.[21] Like Williams and Hochschild, Chua finds a singular white working-class subject straight from the set of the sitcom *Roseanne*. This "tribe," uniform in its outlook and aspirations, stands opposed to the coastal elites, another distinctive tribal group defined by its "disdain for the provincial, the plebian, the patriotic." Chua's "working class" not only detests cosmopolitans, it also resents the privileged troublemakers who claim to speak for the 99 percent. She writes, "It's not just that working-class Americans did not participate in Occupy; many, if not most of them intensely dislike and spurn activist movements." As her primary evidence of working class disdain for "activism," she offers a quote from an essay written by a student lamenting "when elites protest on behalf of us poor people."[22]

These accounts have now become the dominant interpretation of U.S. political division and conflict since Trump's election. Together with scores of other commentators, like the *New York Times* columnists Thomas Edsall and David Brooks,[23] they continually reproduce narratives of cultural alienation and intractable worldviews that underlie contemporary political antagonisms. Shifting material forces, contexts, and interests disappear, as do any genealogies of power, authority, and resistance that might have shaped such dispositions. Racial identifications become severed from the conditions that mediate their production; class identifi-cations become severed from the mediations of white supremacy and racial hierarchy.

These dynamics were also made visible in the reaction on social media by some liberals to the takeover of the Malheur National Wildlife Refuge, who described the occupiers as #Yall-Qaeda, #VanillaIsis, #YeeHawdist, and #YokelHaram. The work of racial transposition here is clear, as anti-Islamic signifiers become attached to caricatured descriptions of "white trash."[24] As we explored in chapter 5, the occupation and the white-producerist and settler-colonial language that it deployed demand serious political analysis and critique; the authoritarian and nationalist vision they advance cannot be underestimated. But the mockery and disdain used here mirrors the same characterizations made by J. D. Vance, Charles Murray, and the *National Review*'s Kevin Williamson, in which cultural dysfunction and parochialism lie at the heart of social conflicts.

For all of these authors and commentators, political interests and worldviews are fixed and unitary; they are the expression of primordial cultural (or tribal) worlds and attachments, seemingly exogenous to the terrain of political struggle. Political conscious-ness and identification itself is removed from social struggle and mediation. It is an argument for a kind of political and cultural hereditarianism in which the best we can do, as Chua urges in her epilogue, is to hold cross-cultural potlucks and movie nights that will "allow ourselves to see our tribal adversaries as fellow Amer-icans" so that we can realize that "what holds the United States together is the American Dream."[25]

Such appeals to civic nationalism and cultural pluralism will not address the complicated and intensified forms of domination and exploitation that underlie the cases examined in this book. As Phil A. Neel argues in his book *Hinterland: America's New Land-scape of Class and Conflict*, the zones of economic neglect outside the metropolitan centers of capital will continue to increase in area as infrastructure, social connection, and economic viability collapse.[26] But if we treat class and race as self-contained cate-gories, we miss their protean nature and dynamic co-constitution.

The analysis we laid out in this book is focused on actors seeking to forge new identifications by reconfiguring the politics of both race and class. Figures like Kay Coles James, Steve Bannon, and Joey Gibson creatively attempt to reconfigure political identities through the incorporation of civil rights discourses. Meanwhile, neoliberal elites and their intellectual promoters like Charles Murray and Kevin Williamson employ old racist tropes to justify the economic abandonment of white workers and the poor. Theirs is hardly a static world. They understand and take seriously the contingency of political identification and the ways that race can signal new configurations of political power.

"Some of the Most Dangerous Work You Can Do"

How, then, might *we* begin to reimagine the relationship between race and class in ways that disrupt tired appeals to the white working class on the one hand or superficial appeals to identity politics on the other? There are in fact many examples that anticipate the flourishing of social movements rooted in a dynamic understanding of political interests and contingent identifications, in perspectives committed to building solidarities and alliances through shared struggle and collective engagement.

On December 4, 1967, Dr. Martin Luther King Jr. announced that the following spring, his Southern Christian Leadership Conference would "lead waves of the nation's poor and disinherited to Washington D.C." to demand "jobs and income for all." King described a nation "gorged on money while millions of its citizens are denied a good education, adequate health services, decent housing, meaningful employment, and even respect, and are then told to be responsible." While the "true responsibility for the existence of these deplorable conditions lies ultimately with the larger society" it was the "federal government that had the power to act, the resources to tap, and the duty to respond."[27]

The Poor People's Campaign would take aim at what King had condemned earlier that year as the "giant triplets of racism, materialism, and militarism." They demanded an expansive state premised on a recognition of the interdependence of everyone in the polity, rejecting the myths of settler sovereignty, autonomy, and producerism. If, as King argued, our lives are interdependent, then we are all, in some sense, parasites—necessarily dependent on one another.[28] It was a vision rooted in long traditions of Black internationalism and social democracy, an archive of analysis and political practice attentive to the ravages of unrestrained market systems that could only be resisted through popular education and mobilization. Racially subordinated groups have had far more experience with and exposure to state violence and unfettered state power then any contemporary "patriot" group. It was the government, after all, that legitimated and sustained chattel slavery and Jim Crow, enforced the genocide, removal, and containment of Native people, implemented racist immigration and internment laws, and repressed antiracist social movements. Yet informed by these experiences, King could still imagine a robust state that could be mobilized in service of emancipation rather than repression, one rooted in a vision of social protection and redistribution. This framework was born out of Black struggle and experience, yet its liberatory commitments were sweeping. The effort, King predicted, would draw "representatives of the millions of non-Negro poor—Indians, Mexican-Americans, Puerto Ricans, Appalachians and others."[29] These groups had distinct (and internally disparate) experiences of subordination, but they could recognize in one another a shared vision and aspiration for the conditions of their emancipation.

King's assassination five months later and a series of other constraints and missteps prevented the Poor People's Campaign from realizing these transformations.[30] But the assumptions that guided the campaign's vision of building a widespread anti-poverty movement that would draw people from markedly different social locations, experiences, and traditions holds important insights for our time. King did not presume that an alienated or tribal "white working class" would remain forever hostile to the interests or aspirations of Black people who were organizing against their subjugation. Nor did he assume that such connections could only be built through an undifferentiated appeal to class unity or a color-blind "Americanism" that erased distinct experiences of racial domination. King instead imagined alternative forms of political identification that linked the specificity of different social locations to a shared vision of redistribution facilitated through state action.

George Lipsitz has described these new identifications as arising from the "troubling but tremendously important questions about what it means to be allied with the struggles of others [and] about which obligations and responsibilities arise from that difficult yet necessary work."[31] Lipsitz critiques the assumption that social solidarity and collective action "require everyone to be the same." They do not and they cannot. He turns to Kimberlé Crenshaw's work on feminist antiracism to demonstrate that all distinct social formations and groups are characterized by internal hierarchy, difference, and experience. This work of fashioning solidarity from heterogeneous spaces is the labor long emphasized by women-of-color feminisms. As Audre Lorde contends, "unity does not mean unanimity." Instead, the suturing of different identifications requires us to do the "unromantic and tedious work necessary to forge meaningful coalitions . . . recognizing which coalitions are possible and which coalitions are not."[32] Bernice Johnson Reagon has explained that coalition work such as this cannot be done in the comforts of "your home" and within the realm of the familiar. "Coalition work has to be done in the streets. And it is some of the most dangerous work you can do. And you shouldn't look for comfort."[33]

Reagon, Lorde, and other feminists of color emphasize a tradition of collective learning and a capacity to incorporate fractured, diverse, and changing conditions. "One of the most basic Black survival skills," writes Lorde, "is the ability to change, to metabolize experience, good or ill, into something that is useful, lasting, effective." Thus "the necessary ingredient needed to make the past work for the future is our energy in the present, metabolizing one into the other."[34]

Lipsitz insists that in practice such "alliances emerge from the processes of struggle, not prior to it." For King and the Poor People's Campaign, this meant that "working for social change entailed working sometimes with people who are unlikeable. It meant finding ways to turn bitter enemies into unwitting architects of our own liberation." These efforts would move us "beyond the obvious organic and proximate affinities and affiliations to envision and enact" broader political worlds and policies.[35]

An analysis that treats the social distinctions and antagonisms visible in any one period as permanent and inevitable will only lead to despair. If we require an undifferentiated unity to sustain oppositional social movements, then we are destined to fail. Lorde insists that "our struggles are particular, but we are not alone."[36] As Fred Moten has described it in the context of white identification with Black power struggles, "The problematic of coalition is that coalition isn't something that emerges so that you can come help me, a maneuver that always gets traced back to your own interests. The coalition emerges out of your recognition that it's fucked up for you, in the same way that we've already recognized that it's fucked up for us. I don't need your help. I just need you to recognize that this shit is killing you, too, however much more softly, you stupid motherfucker, you know?"[37] Moten's use of the term "recognition" here is instructive. How might people from diverse social locations, experiences, and histories not only come to recognize these shared conditions and structures of deprivation but also come to recognize in one another the capacity to labor together to build new futures? And how might those marked as white recognize in their precarity the origins and structures of a system predicated on the death of racialized others?

There are examples of the kind of solidarity amid difference that are rooted in precisely the kind of intersectional and multi-issue frameworks theorized by King, Lorde, Lipsitz, Crenshaw, and so many others. In the same areas of rural Oregon that have become the focus of militia and patriot groups like those led by Ammon Bundy, an organization called the Rural Organizing Project (ROP) has been working to link the experiences, aspirations, and energies of diverse communities that struggle against economic privation and state abandonment and violence. The group started as a loosely connected network of mostly white rural residents who mobilized to defeat a series of anti-gay ballot measures sponsored by the conservative Christian Coalition in the late 1980s and early 1990s. Like the militia and patriot groups, those right-wing Evangelicals sought to connect an offer of homophobic and patriarchal policy measures as a response to growing forms of precarity brought about by the decline in the region's timber industry and broader economy.[38]

From its origins, ROP understood the interdependence of race and class. But its members did not presume that one's social location automatically dictated one's politics or aligned one with a "political tribe." These are precisely the allegiances to be won and the identifications to be secured. ROP's organizing model is rooted in the possibility of building such identifications through shared struggle and reflection. It has hosted political education discussions in rural communities across the state on the histories of anti-Black racism and exclusion. Its members—immigrant and non-immigrant alike—have mobilized to support hunger strikes led by detainees at the Northern Oregon Regional Correctional Facility to protest the inhumane conditions facing immigrant refugee detainees there. Their economic justice work focuses on linking the interests and needs of abandoned rural communities with those of Native American tribal governments, immigrant rights groups, and urban organizations led by people of color. When militia and patriot groups have formed around anti-statist and authoritarian projects, they have organized counter-mobilizations to link issues of rural economic and social precarity to broader histories of racial exclusion and corporate resource extraction.[39]

ROP is among dozens of rural-based organizations, many with decades of organizing experience, whose work is premised on the belief that political identifications are always being made and remade. Against the chorus of commentators who imagine a cocooned white working class bound by its atavistic "folkways," their organizing is responsive to the complexity of experiences, problems, and political histories in rural areas and the opportunities to articulate these issues within broad-based political formations.[40] This is the "dangerous work" described by Bernice Reagon that is necessary to illuminate new futures.

Following these examples, what would it mean to rebel against the conditions wrought by economic collapse and abandonment and by overweening state power without holding on to settler-colonial and white racial myths about individual autonomy? What would make it possible to see both the similarities and differences with state brutality and neoliberal rapacity in Flint, Ferguson, and the towns and cities of post–Hurricane Maria Puerto Rico?

Currently, habits of scripted position taking all too often stand in for analysis, making the possibilities of resistance less imaginable. A liberal antiracism that is focused entirely on personal microaggressions or the lack of diversity in corporate boardrooms, universities, and the culture industry forecloses the possibility of critique necessary to attack the roots of racial disparities in wealth, income, life expectancy, education, housing, and employment. At the same time, a class politics that merely calls for universal programs—or worse, one that attacks antiracism because it is seen to be alienating to white workers—is not capable of battling the racialized politics that has always made possible capitalist domination, and intensifies it today.

This much is clear: race—whether in the form of neoliberal multiculturalism, far-right authoritarianism, or claims about cultural and genetic fitness—will continue to be pressed into service by those who wish to solidify and extend the extreme political and economic hierarchies that foster human misery and planetary destruction. We must match the extraordinary flexibility of these new racializations with dexterity in our own analysis and action. The only anchor should be our commitment to emancipation.

ACKNOWLEDGMENTS

The Guyanese-born theorist Walter Rodney insisted that "new questions" are often demanded by "our predicament at the present time." In the course of collaboratively writing this book over seven years, the predicaments of our times have mounted, and so have our questions. We thank the many interlocutors who helped us think through such questions, even when we had few answers.

We began thinking about this project in the wake of the 2010 midterm elections and the sudden escalation in attacks on public-sector unions and the parallel emergence of a new cadre of people of color within deeply conservative formations. We are thankful to have been able to share this work with colleagues at the Alliance for a Just Society; the Labor Research Colloquium, coordinated by Gordon Lafer and the University of Oregon Labor Education and Research Center; "Race, Law, and the American State: An Interdisciplinary Symposium" at University of Michigan Law School, cohosted by Matthew Lassiter and William Novak; annual meetings of the Western Political Science Association and the Social Science History Association; and the staff at the Service Employees International Union 1199NE. We thank *American Quarterly* editor Mari Yoshihara and several anonymous reviewers for invaluable feedback in strengthening our chapter on public-sector workers.

We thank Roopali Mukherjee, Sarah Banet-Weiser, and Herman Gray for including our essay "Theorizing Race in the Age of

Inequality," which draws from several chapters in this book, in their coedited volume *Racism Postrace*, as well as the feedback we received during the review process.

We presented versions of chapter 4 at the "Trump's America" conference at the University College Dublin's Clinton Institute in April 2017, as well as at the Ethnicity, Race, and Migration colloquium at Yale University. Participants in the 2017 African American Policy Forum Social Justice Writers Retreat, including Devon Carbado, Kimberlé Crenshaw, Barbara Arnwine, Ezra Young, Leah Goodridge, Jason Wu, Taneisha Means, Luke Harris, Sumi Cho, and Priscilla Yamin, provided generative feedback on a preliminary version of the Introduction. We also thank the Whiteness in the Americas Working Group convened by Carlos Vargas-Ramos and Ana Ramos-Zayas for workshopping chapter 2.

At the University of Minnesota Press, our editor, Pieter Martin, has been a thoughtful and engaged presence from the start, encouraging us to continue to develop the manuscript even as the conditions and forces we were writing about seemed to be changing daily. Lester Spence, Cristina Beltrán, and an anonymous reviewer selected by the Press offered generous and productive feedback on the first version of the manuscript; we are indebted for their careful engagement with our arguments and aspirations.

At different phases of the project we received advice, ideas, and inspiration from George Schulman, Peter Walker, Steve Beda, Raahi Reddy, Spencer Sunshine, George Lipsitz, Daria Roithmayr, Priscilla Yamin, Laura Pulido, Rachael Bowen, Loren Kajikawa, Norma Martinez-HoSang, and the late Sandi Morgen. Our experiences serving on the Organizing Committee and Executive Council of the faculty union at the University of Oregon, United Academics, AAUP/AFT Local 3209, AFL-CIO, helped us to think in concrete ways about the attacks on public-sector workers and the resistance that such attacks can inspire.

At the eleventh hour, the work of research assistant Karen Marks allowed us to meet our deadlines. We also thank the University of Oregon's Department of Political Science and Department of Ethnic Studies and Yale University's American Studies and Ethnicity, Race, and Migration units for funding and support that made this book possible. For permission to republish photographs, we acknowledge Peter Walker, Jessica Campbell and the Rural Organizing Project, and Sam Schaffer.

Collaborative intellectual projects depend on trust, generosity, and shared political groundings. These qualities have never been in short supply in our friendship and writing partnership, and they helped strengthen this book at every turn. Our families have endured our obsession with this project and its long timeline. Thank you to Ben, Adam, Priscilla, Norma, Isaac, Umai, and Pablo, for everything.

NOTES

Introduction

    1. Joey Gibson, interview with the authors, April 29, 2018. Gibson lost the Republican primary in early August, garnering less than 3 percent of the vote. "Cantwell, Hutchison Advance in Senate Race; Joey Gibson Loses Big," Oregon Live, August 7, 2018, https://www.oregon live.com/pacific-northwest-news/index.ssf/2018/08/cantwell_hutchison_ advance_in.html.

    2. Katie Shepard, "Police in Vancouver Arrest Man for Nearly Running Down Antifa Protesters with His Truck," *Willamette Week*, September 10, 2017; Patrick May, "Who's behind This Weekend's Right-Wing Rally at Crissy Field?" *San Jose Mercury News*, August 23, 2017; "14 Arrested as Pro-Trump Rally Draws Massive Counter-protests in Portland," *Chicago Tribune*, June 4, 2017.

    3. Jason Wilson, "Portland Knife Attack: Tension High as 'Free Speech Rally' Set for Weekend," *Guardian*, May 29, 2017.

    4. Jason Wilson, "How a Gun-Carrying, Far-Right Activist Plots a Run at the US Senate," *Guardian,* June 3, 2018. Our analysis of Gibson and Patriot Prayer is informed by our interview with Gibson, observation of several far-right and militia rallies in the Northwest in 2016 and 2017, and discussions with journalists Jason Wilson and Arun Gupta, who have covered Gibson and Patriot Prayer closely.

    5. See, for example, the images and videos gathered in "Unite the Right, Patriot Prayer, Joey Gibson, and the Proud Boys," It's Going Down, August 2, 2018, https://itsgoingdown.org/unite-the-right-patriot-prayer -joey-gibson-the-proud-boys/, and by journalist Arun Gupta, https://twit ter.com/arunindy?lang=en.

6. Jonathan Cohn, "Why Public Employees are the New Welfare Queens," *New Republic*, August 8, 2010, https://newrepublic.com/article/76884/why-your-fireman-has-better-pension-you; Joshua Holland, "Public Employees: The 21st Century's Welfare Queens," *Pittsburgh Post-Gazette*, November 14, 2010; Randy Albelda, "Teachers, Secretaries, and Social Workers: The New Welfare Moms?" *Dollars & Sense*, May/June 2011, 6–17.

7. Larry Bartels, *Unequal Democracy: The Political Economy of the New Gilded Age* (New York: Sage, 2018).

8. "Wealth by Decile," Survey of Consumer Finances 2016, Federal Reserve System, https://www.federalreserve.gov/econres/scfindex.htm.

9. Quoted in George Lipsitz, *The Possessive Investment in Whiteness: How White People Profit from Identity Politics* (Philadelphia: Temple University Press, 1998), 183.

10. Timothy Sandefur, *Frederick Douglass: Self-Made Man* (Santa Monica: Cato, 2018). See also David W. Blight, "How the Right Co-opts Frederick Douglass," *New York Times*, February 13, 2018. Blight writes: "At the unveiling ceremony for the statue of Douglass in the United States Capitol in 2013, congressional Republicans proudly wore large buttons that read, 'Frederick Douglass Was a Republican.' Douglass's descendants who were there, as well as scholars like me with, shall we say, different training, smiled and endured."

11. Stuart Hall and Doreen Massey, "Interpreting the Crisis," *Soundings*, no. 44 (Spring 2010): 64.

12. Antonio Gramsci, *Selections from the Prison Notebooks* (London: Lawrence and Wishart, 1971); Stuart Hall, "Race, Articulation and Societies Structured in Dominance," in *Sociological Theories: Race and Colonialism* (Paris: UNESCO, 1980), 305–45. Attention to a new conjuncture does not mean, in Hall's terms, "the substitution of one mode for another." Earlier formations "have not and cannot possibly disappear." Instead, new developments and modes of conflict do "to some degree displace, reorganize and reposition the different cultural strategies in relation to one another." Stuart Hall, "New Ethnicities," in *Stuart Hall: Critical Dialogues in Cultural Studies,* ed. Kuan-Hsing Chen and David Morley (London: Routledge, 1996), 442.

13. The rise in organized white-supremacist activity preceded the Trump campaign and presidency. See, for example, U.S. Department of Homeland Security, *Rightwing Extremism: Current Economic and Political Climate Fueling Resurgence in Radicalization and Recruitment*, April 7, 2009, https://fas.org/irp/eprint/rightwing.pdf.

14. Laura Smith Park, "UN Warns United States over Racist Rhetoric," CNN, August 23, 2017.

15. W. E. B. Du Bois, *Black Reconstruction in America: An Essay toward a History of the Part Which Black Folk Played in an Attempt to Reconstruct Democracy in America, 1860–1880* (New York: Harcourt, Brace, 1935).

16. Adolph Reed and Merlin Chowkwanyun, "Race, Class, Crisis: The Discourse of Racial Disparities and Its Analytical Discontents," *Socialist Register* 48 (2012): 48.

17. Barbara Fields and Karen Fields, *Racecraft: The Soul of Inequality in American Life* (London: Verso, 2012), 18.

18. Adolph Reed Jr., "Splendors and Miseries of the Antiracist 'Left,'" November 6, 2016, https://nonsite.org/editorial/splendors-and-miseries-of-the-antiracist-left-2.

19. Jacqueline Jones, *A Dreadful Deceit: The Myth of Race from the Colonial Era to Obama's America* (New York: Basic Books, 2013), x.

20. Hall, "Race, Articulation," 342.

21. Hall, "Race, Articulation," 341.

22. Hall, "Race, Articulation," 342.

23. Ruth Wilson Gilmore, "The Worrying State of the Anti-prison Movement," *Social Justice,* February 23, 2015.

24. Lisa Duggan, *The Twilight of Equality* (Boston: Beacon Press, 2002), xvi.

25. Jodi Melamed, "The Spirit of Neoliberalism: From Racial Liberalism to Neoliberal Multiculturalism," *Social Text* 24, no. 4 (2006): 1.

26. Melamed, "The Spirit of Neoliberalism," 14.

27. Simon Marginson, *The Dream Is Over: The Crisis of Clark Kerr's California Idea of Higher Education* (Oakland: University of California Press, 2016).

28. James Baldwin, "The Fire Next Time: Letter to My Nephew," in *The Price of the Ticket,* ed. James Baldwin (New York: St. Martin's/ Marek, 1985), 334.

29. Natalia Molina, *How Race Is Made in America* (Berkeley: University of California Press, 2014), 6. If Molina's racial scripts describe the content or substance of particular racializations, racial transposition refers to the process by which elements of those scripts move from one group to another.

30. As Hall put it, race "floats" as a political signifier, and its meaning is subject to ongoing political struggle. Hall, "Race, Articulation."

31. Cedric Robinson, *Black Marxism: The Making of The Black Radical Tradition* (Chapel Hill: University of North Carolina Press, 2000), 26.

32. Molina, *How Race Is Made in America*, introduction. See also Natalia Molina, Daniel Martinez HoSang, and Ramon Gutiérrez, eds., *Relational Formations of Race: Theory, Method, and Practice* (Oakland: University of California Press, 2019).

33. Dara Lind, "Trump on Deported Immigrants: 'They're Not People. They're Animals,'" *Vox*, May 17, 2018.

34. On these origins and connections, see Khalil Gibran Muhammad, *The Condemnation of Blackness: Race, Crime, and the Making of Modern Urban America* (Cambridge, Mass.: Harvard University Press, 2011); Kelly Lytle Hernández, "Amnesty or Abolition?" *Boom: A Journal of California* 1, no. 4 (Winter 2011): 54–68; and Patrisia Macías-Rojas, *From Deportation to Prison: The Politics of Immigration Enforcement in Post–Civil Rights America* (New York: New York University Press, 2016).

35. Tiffany Willoughby-Herard, *Waste of a White Skin: The Carnegie Corporation and the Racial Logic of White Vulnerability* (Berkeley: University of California Press, 2015), 1.

1. *"Parasites of Government"*

1. Rush Limbaugh, "Union Thugs: 'Raise My Taxes!'" *The Rush Limbaugh Show*, May 19, 2011.

2. Rush Limbaugh, "We've Reached the Tipping Point," *The Rush Limbaugh Show*, February 18, 2011.

3. Steven Greenhouse, "Strained States Turning to Laws to Curb Labor Unions," *New York Times*, January 3, 2011.

4. Ben Smith and Maggie Haberman, "Pols Turn on Labor Unions," *Politico*, June 6, 2010. See also Joseph McCartin, "Convenient Scapegoat: Public Workers under Assault," *Dissent*, Spring 2011, https://www.dissentmagazine.org/article/convenient-scapegoat-public-workers-under-assault.

5. Chip Berlet and Matthew N. Lyons, *Right-Wing Populism in America: Too Close for Comfort* (New York: Guilford Press, 2000); Linda Gordon and Nancy Fraser, "A Genealogy of Dependency: Tracing a Keyword of the U.S. Welfare State," *Signs* 19, no. 2 (1994): 309–36.

6. Jill Quadagno, *The Color of Welfare: How Racism Undermined the War on Poverty* (Oxford: Oxford University Press, 1994); Ange-Marie Hancock, *The Politics of Disgust: The Public Identity of the Welfare Queen* (New York: New York University Press, 2004); Elena R. Gutiérrez,

Fertile Matters: The Politics of Mexican-Origin Women's Reproduction (Austin: University of Texas Press, 2008).

7. David Cooper, Mark Gable, and Algernon Austin, "The Public-Sector Jobs Crisis," in *EPI Briefing Paper* (Washington, D.C.: Economic Policy Institute, 2012).

8. Hannah Walker and Dylan Bennett, "The Whiteness of Wisconsin's Wages: Racial Geography and the Defeat of Public Sector Labor Unions in Wisconsin," *New Political Science* 37, no. 2 (2015): 191.

9. Tim Pawlenty, "Government Unions vs. Taxpayers," *Wall Street Journal*, December 13, 2010.

10. Following the 2010 elections, the National Conference of State Legislatures reported a significant increase in legislative proposals at the state level seeking to restrict collective bargaining rights and weaken unions. Peter Rachleff, "The Right-to-Work Offensive: Tracking the Spread of the Anti-union Virus," *New Labor Forum* 21, no. 1 (2012): 22–29; Richard B. Freeman and Eunice Han, "The War against Public Sector Collective Bargaining in the US," *Journal of Industrial Relations* 54, no. 3 (2012): 393.

11. M. Jaqui Alexander, *Pedagogies of Crossing: Meditations on Feminism, Sexual Politics, Memory, and the Sacred* (Durham: Duke University Press, 2006), 99.

12. We build on the work of other scholars who have demonstrated that there have never been separate systems of race and class in the United States, and that indeed capitalism and racial domination have been historically coterminous. See, for instance, Edward Baptist, *The Half That Has Never Been Told: Slavery and the Making of American Capitalism* (New York: Basic Books, 2014); Robin D. G. Kelley, *Hammer and Hoe: Alabama Communists during the Great Depression* (Chapel Hill: University of North Carolina Press, 1990); Adolph Reed, "Unraveling the Relation of Race and Class in American Politics," in *Political Power and Social Theory*, vol. 15, ed. Diane E. Davis (West Yorkshire: Emerald Group Publishing Limited, Adolph Reed), 265–74; and Cedric Robinson, *Black Marxism: The Making of the Black Radical Tradition* (Chapel Hill: University of North Carolina Press, 2000).

13. Ira Katznelson, *When Affirmative Action Was White: An Untold History of Racial Inequality in Twentieth-Century America* (New York: Norton, 2005). See also Jonathan Cohn, "Why Public Employees Are the New Welfare Queens," *New Republic*, August 7, 2010, https://newrepublic.com/article/76884/why-your-fireman-has-better-pension-you.

14. Steve Fraser and Joshua B. Freeman, "In the Rearview Mirror: A Brief History of Opposition to Public Sector Unionism," *New Labor Forum* 20, no. 3 (2011): 93–96.

15. Nelson Lichtenstein and Elizabeth Tandy Shermer, "Introduction," in *The Right and Labor in America: Politics, Ideology, and Imagination*, ed. Nelson Lichtenstein and Elizabeth Tandy Shermer (Philadelphia: University of Pennsylvania Press, 2012), 8. See also Joseph McCartin and Jean-Christian Vinel, "Compulsory Unionism: Sylvester Petro and the Career of an Anti-union Idea," in Lichtenstein and Shermer, *The Right and Labor in America*, 226–51.

16. See, for example, Don Bellante and James Long, "The Political Economy of the Rent-Seeking Society: The Case of Public Employees and Their Unions," *Journal of Labor Research* 2, no. 1 (1981): 1–14.

17. Lichtenstein and Shermer, *The Right and Labor in America*, 3–4.

18. Steven Greenhut, "Out of the Way, Peasants," *Orange County Register*, April 20, 2008.

19. Steven Greenhut, *Plunder! How Public Employee Unions Are Raiding Treasuries, Controlling Our Lives, and Bankrupting the Nation* (Santa Ana, Calif.: Forum Press, 2009), 3. Other conservative critiques of public-sector unions include Daniel DiSalvo, *Government Unions and the Bankrupting of America* (New York: Encounter Books, 2011); and Mallory Factor, *Shadowbosses: Government Unions Control America and Rob Taxpayers Blind* (New York: Center Street, 2012).

20. Four years after signing Act 10, the 2011 legislation that weakened public-sector unions, Walker signed much broader "right to work" legislation that affected both public-sector and private-sector unions. Craig Gilbert, "Walker's Support of Right to Work Could Alter Union Equation," *Milwaukee Journal Sentinel*, March 4, 2015.

21. Limbaugh, "Union Thugs."

22. Berlet and Lyons, *Right-Wing Populism*.

23. Ruth Wilson Gilmore, *Golden Gulag: Prisons, Surplus, Crisis, and Opposition in Globalizing California* (Berkeley: University of California Press, 2006).

24. Walker and Bennett, "The Whiteness of Wisconsin's Wages"; Dan Kaufman, "Scott Walker and the Fate of the Union," *New York Times Magazine*, June 14, 2015, https://www.nytimes.com/2015/06/14/magazine/scott-walker-and-the-fate-of-the-union.html.

25. David Corn, "SECRET VIDEO: Romney Tells Millionaire Donors What He Really Thinks of Obama Voters," *Mother Jones*, September 18, 2012, http://www.motherjones.com/politics/2012/09/secret-video-private-romney-fundraiser.

26. Alexander Saxton, *The Rise and Fall of the White Republic: Class Politics and Mass Culture in Nineteenth-Century America* (New York: Verso, 1990); Michael Kazin, *The Populist Persuasion: An American History* (Ithaca: Cornell University Press, 1998).

27. Ralph Chaplin, *Wobbly: The Rough-and-Tumble Story of an American Radical* (Chicago: University of Chicago Press, 1948), 167–68.

28. J. Sakai, *Settlers: The Mythology of the White Proletariat,* 3rd ed. (Chicago: Morningstar Press, 1989), chapter 2. For a discussion of this work, see Daniel Berger, "Subjugated Knowledges: Activism, Scholarship, and Ethnic Studies Ways of Knowing," in *Critical Ethnic Studies: A Reader,* ed. Critical Ethnic Studies Editorial Collective (Durham: Duke University Press, 2016), 215–30.

29. Dan Carter, *From George Wallace to Newt Gingrich: Race in the Conservative Counterrevolution, 1963–1994* (Baton Rouge: Louisiana State University Press, 1996); Joseph E. Lowndes, *From the New Deal to the New Right: Race and the Southern Origins of Modern Conservatism* (New Haven, Conn.: Yale University Press, 2008).

30. Thomas Byrne Edsall and Mary D. Edsall, *Chain Reaction: The Impact of Race, Rights, and Taxes on American Politics* (New York: Norton, 1992); Todd Gitlin, *The Twilight of Common Dreams: Why America Is Wracked with Culture Wars* (New York: Holt, 1996).

31. David R. Roediger, *The Wages of Whiteness: Race and the Making of the American Working Class* (New York: Verso, 1999); Eric Lott, *Love and Theft: Blackface Minstrelsy and the American Working Class* (Oxford: Oxford University Press, 1993); Michael Rogin, *Blackface, White Noise: Jewish Immigrants in the Hollywood Melting Pot* (Berkeley: University of California Press, 1998).

32. Daniel HoSang, *Racial Propositions: Ballot Initiatives and the Making of Postwar California* (Berkeley: University of California Press, 2010).

33. For a genealogy of racial anti-statism, see Lowndes, *From the New Deal to the New Right*; for its contemporary effects, see Ian Haney-Lopez, *Dog Whistle Politics: How Coded Racial Appeals Have Reinvented Racism and Wrecked the Middle Class* (Oxford: Oxford University Press, 2014).

34. On the populist tax revolt in California and its relationship to tax cuts for corporations and the wealthy, see Gilmore, *Golden Gulag*; Isaac Martin, *The Permanent Tax Revolt: How the Property Tax Transformed American Politics* (Stanford: Stanford University Press, 2008); and Kitty Calavita, "The New Politics of Immigration: 'Balanced Budget

Conservatism' and the Symbolism of Proposition 187," *Social Problems* 43, no. 3 (1996): 284–305.

35. Patricia Cohen and Robert Gebeloff, "Public Servants Are Losing Their Foothold in the Middle Class," *New York Times,* April 22, 2018.

36. Ruth Milkman and Stephanie Luce, *The State of the Unions 2015: A Profile of Organized Labor in New York City, New York State, and the United States* (New York: John S. Murphy Institute for Worker Education and Labor Studies, 2015).

37. Cooper, Gable, and Austin, "The Public-Sector Jobs Crisis."

38. Jennifer Laird, *Still an Equal Opportunity Employer? Public Sector Employment Inequality after the Great Recession* (Seattle: University of Washington, 2015).

39. Peter Stallybrass and Allon White, *The Politics and Poetics of Transgression* (London: Methuen, 1986).

40. Micah Uetricht, *Strike for America: Chicago Teachers against Austerity* (New York: Verso Press, 2014).

41. Lisa Benson, "What Do We Want? We Want More!!" September 12, 2012, townhall.com/political-cartoons/lisabenson/2012/09/12/103371.

42. "Chicago Teachers Union President Karen Lewis Wants to Eat Your Children. With Cheese and Bacon," *Chicago News Bench*, September 12, 2012, rogersparkbench.blogspot.com/2012/09/chicago-teachers-union-president-karen.html.

43. Anne Norton, *Republic of Signs* (Chicago: University of Chicago Press, 1993).

44. Michelle Malkin, "Chicago Thuggery Personified: Meet Chicago Teachers' Union President Karen Lewis," September 10, 2012, http://michellemalkin.com/2012/09/10/chicago-thuggery-personified-meet-chicago-teachers-union-president-karen-lewis/; Michelle Malkin, "'A' Is for Agitation," September 12, 2012, https://www.nationalreview.com/2012/09/agitation-michelle-malkin/.

45. "Embarassing Video: Chicago Teacher's Union President Karen Lewis Attacks Arne Duncan's 'Lisp,' Jokes about Using Drugs," *Chicago News Report*, November 14, 2011.

46. Comments from YouTube video, "EAGnews.org: CTU President Karen Lewis Uncensored—NSFW," October 1, 2011, www.youtube.com/all_comments?v=A1YXOSaMZzs.

47. Sewell Chan and Jeremy W. Peters, "Chimp-Stimulus Cartoon Raises Racism Concerns," *City Room* (blog), *New York Times*, February 19, 2009.

48. Sean Delonas, "You're Just Gonna Have to Tighten Your Belt," *City Journal*, Spring 2010, city-journal.org/2010/20_2_california-unions.html.

49. Mike Lester, "This Is What Democra-(urp!!)cy Looks Like," March 6, 2011, www.rn-t.com/view/full_story/12168612/article-Mike-Lester-s-Cartoon-03-06-11.

50. *Saturday Night Live*, season 35, episode 20, April 24, 2010.

51. Marilyn V. Yarbrough and Crystal Bennett, "Cassandra and the 'Sistahs': The Peculiar Treatment of African American Women in the Myth of Women as Liars," *Journal of Gender, Race and Justice* 3, no. 2 (2000): 626–27.

52. Alexander, *Pedagogies of Crossing*, 100.

53. AFP California, "'Common Sense': Lifestyles of the Rich & Famous on Government Pensions," YouTube, 2010, www.youtube.com/watch?v=JsVGpJTup9U.

54. AFP California, "Lifeguards Make $200,000/Retire at Age 50 Exposed on Inside Edition with David Spady," 2012, video file in authors' possession. See also David Spady, "$200,000 Lifeguards to Receive Millions in Retirement," Townhall.com, May 8, 2011, https://townhall.com/columnists/davidspady/2011/05/08/$200,000-lifeguards-to-receive-millions-in-retirement-n947640.

55. Emily Foxhall and Jeremiah Dobruck, "Newport Beach Considers Outsourcing Lifeguard Services to Cut Costs," *Los Angeles Times*, January 6, 2014.

56. Michael Scott, "Issue 2 Defeated: Million Votes Are in and 63 Percent Say No, AP Says," *Cleveland-Plain Dealer*, November 8, 2011.

57. Konrad Yakabuski, "Battle Rages over Ohio's Union-Limiting Law," *Globe and Mail* (Canada), October 29, 2011.

58. Fox WUPW, "John Kasich Discusses Issue 2," September 29, 2011, 56.

59. Joe Vardon, "Group Raised $42.2 Million in Campaign against Issue 2," *Columbus Dispatch*, December 16, 2011.

60. Ads are archived on the website of the campaign consultant, The New Media Firm, https://thenewmediafirm.com/portfolio/.

61. WDTNTV, "'Ohio Firefighters Release Ad about Issue 2," September 2, 2011, 12–13.

62. These and similar ads are archived on YouTube, https://www.youtube.com/user/WeAreOhio/videos.

63. For theoretical and methodological considerations relevant to the visual culture and union strategy, see Janis Bailey and Di McAtee,

"The Politics and Poetics of Union Transgression: The Role of Visual Methods in Analyzing Union Protest Strategy," *Social Analysis* 47, no. 3 (2003): 27–45.

64. See Staughton Lynd, *Solidarity Unionism: Rebuilding the Labor Movement from Below* (Oakland, Calif.: PM Press, 2015); and Thomas Geoghegan, *Only One Thing Can Save Us: Why America Needs a New Kind of Labor Movement* (New York: The New Press, 2014).

65. Dana Frank, *Buy American: The Untold Story of Economic Nationalism* (Boston: Beacon Press, 1999).

66. The cases include *Harris v. Quinn*, 573 U.S. ___ (2014) and *Friedrichs v. California Teachers Association*, 578 U.S. ___ (2016).

67. Critics of Walker and other anti-union figures pointed to the many tax breaks and subsidies given to wealthy individuals and corporations that increased state and local budget deficits and the tax burdens of middle- and low-income households. Kaufman, "Scott Walker."

68. Comment posted on Senator Silk's Facebook page on March 29, 2018, https://www.facebook.com/senatorjosephsilk/; Victoria Pasquantonio, "What You Need to Know about the Oklahoma Teacher Walkout," *PBS Newshour*, April 2, 1018.

69. Mary Papenfuss, "Kentucky Gov. Apologizes after Claiming Teacher Protest Would Result in Child Abuse," *Huffington Post*, April 13, 2018.

70. Micah Uetricht, *Strike for America: Chicago Teachers against Austerity* (New York: Verso Press, 2014).

71. Jane McAlevey, "The West Virginia Teachers Strike Shows That Winning Big Requires Creating a Crisis," *The Nation*, March 12, 2018.

72. Matt Pearce, "Red-State Revolt Continues: Teachers Strike in Oklahoma and Protest in Kentucky," *Los Angeles Times*, April 2, 2018.

73. Amy Chua, *Political Tribes: Group Instinct and the Fate of Nations* (New York: Penguin, 2018); Thomas Edsall, "Which Side Are You On?" *New York Times*, May 10, 2018.

2. "The Incomprehensible Malice—of Poor White America"

1. Janelle Jones, "The Racial Wealth Gap," *Working Economics Blog*, February 13, 2017; Chuck Collins, Dedrick Asante-Muhammed, Emanuel Nieves, and Josh Hoxie, "The Road to Zero Wealth," *Institute for Policy Studies*, September 11, 2017. See also Raj Chetty, Nathaniel Hendren, Maggie R. Jones, and Sonya R. Porter, "Race and Economic Opportunity in the United States: An Intergenerational Perspective," National Bureau of Economic Research Working Paper No. 24441, March 2018.

2. Adolph Reed Jr., "Du Bois and the 'Wages of Whiteness': What He Meant, What He Didn't, and Besides, It Shouldn't Matter for Our Politics Anyway," Nonsite.org, June 29, 2017.

3. Ira Katznelson, *When Affirmative Action Was White: An Untold History of Racial Inequality in Twentieth-Century America* (New York: Norton, 2005).

4. David Freund, *Colored Property: State Policy and White Racial Politics in Suburban America* (Chicago: University of Chicago Press, 2007).

5. M. F. Jacobson, *Whiteness of a Different Color: European Immigrants and the Alchemy of Race* (Cambridge, Mass.: Harvard University Press, 1999).

6. Cheryl Harris, "Whiteness as Property," *Harvard Law Review* 106, no. 8 (1993): 1713.

7. Joel Olson, "Whiteness and the Polarization of American Politics," *Political Research Quarterly* 61, no. 4 (2008): 708.

8. Olson, "Whiteness," 708.

9. Olson, "Whiteness," 709.

10. Keeanga-Yamahtta Taylor, "The White Power Presidency: Race and Class in the Trump Era," *New Political Science* 40 (2018): 111.

11. Tiffany Willoughby-Herard, *Waste of a White Skin: The Carnegie Corporation and the Racial Logic of White Vulnerability* (Berkeley: University of California Press, 2015), 11.

12. James Baldwin, "An Open Letter to My Sister, Miss Angela Davis," *New York Review of Books*, January 7, 1971.

13. John Dominis and Michael Murphy, "The Valley of Poverty," *Life*, January 31, 1964, 54–65. See also Ben Cosgrove, "War on Poverty: Portraits from an Appalachian Battleground, 1964," *Time*, January 7, 2014.

14. See the Robert F. Kennedy Performance Project, rfkineky.org.

15. Elizabeth Catte, *What You Are Getting Wrong about Appalachia* (Cleveland: Belt Publishing, 2018).

16. "A Hand Up, Not a Hand Out!" Sargent Shriver Peace Institute, http://www.sargentshriver.org/blog/empowerment-government-and-the-war-on-poverty.

17. See, for example, Robin Averbeck, *Liberalism Is Not Enough: Race and Poverty in Postwar Political Thought* (Chapel Hill: University of North Carolina Press, 2018).

18. Martin Gilens, *Why Americans Hate Welfare: Race, Media, and the Politics of Antipoverty Policy* (Chicago: University of Chicago Press, 1999); Ange Marie Hancock, *The Politics of Disgust: The Public Identity of the Welfare Queen* (New York: New York University Press, 2004); Jill

Quadagno, *The Color of Welfare* (New York: Oxford University Press, 1994).

19. These figures are from 2014. Jessica L. Semega, Kayla R. Fontenot, and Melissa A. Kollar, *U.S. Census Bureau, Current Population Reports, P60-259, Income and Poverty in the United States: 2016* (Washington, D.C.: Government Printing Office, 2017).

20. Khaing Zaw, Jhumpa Bhattacharya, Anne E. Price, Darrick Hamilton, and William Darity Jr., "Women, Race and Wealth," *Research Brief Series, Volume 1: A Joint Publication with the Insight Center for Community Economic Development* (Durham: Samuel DuBois Cook Center on Social Equity, 2017).

21. Paul Jargowsky, *Architecture of Segregation: Civil Unrest, the Concentration of Poverty, and Public Policy,* The Century Foundation, August 7, 2015.

22. Leonard Pitts Jr., "Poverty Doesn't Have a Skin Color," *Miami Herald*, April 4, 2017.

23. The incarceration rate for white men in 2010 was 678 per 100,000 U.S. residents, a threefold increase since 1960. The rate for African American men in 2010 was 4,347 per 100,000, up from 1,313 per 100,000 U.S. residents in 1960. In 2011 the rate for the United States as a whole was 743 per 100,000 in 2010. In 2011 the country with the next-highest rate was Russia at 577 per 100,000 residents. See Bruce Drake, "Incarceration Gap Widens between Whites and Blacks," September 6, 2013, http://www.pewresearch.org/fact-tank/2013/09/06/incarceration-gap -between-whites-and-blacks-widens/; Peter Wagner, "Incarceration Is Not an Equal Opportunity Punishment," August 28, 2012, https://www.pris onpolicy.org/articles/notequal.html; and International Centre for Prison Studies, "ICPS News Digest 1st Edition," January/February 2011, http:// www.prisonstudies.org/sites/default/files/resources/downloads/icps_ news_digest.pdf. See also Ashley Nellis, "The Color of Justice: Racial and Ethnic Disparity in State Prisons," *The Sentencing Project*, June 14, 2016.

24. Adam Tooze, "Quantifying Incarceration," *Jacobin Magazine*, November 2017.

25. Anne Case and Angus Deaton, "Rising Morbidity and Mortality in Midlife among White Non-Hispanic Americans in the 21st Century," *Proceedings of the National Academy of the Sciences of the United States of America* 112, no. 49 (December 2015): 15078–83.

26. Noli Brazil, "Spatial Variation in the Hispanic Paradox: Mortality Rates in New and Established Hispanic US Destinations," *Population, Space and Place* 23, no. 1 (2017): 23.

27. Anne Case and Angus Deaton, "Mortality and Morbidity in the 21st Century," https://www.brookings.edu/bpea-articles/mortality-and -morbidity-in-the-21st-century/.

28. Carol Graham and Sergio Pinto, "Unequal Hopes and Lives in the U.S.: Optimism, Race, Place, and Premature Mortality," *Journal of Population Economics* 687, no. 6 (January 2018). It should be noted that the same declining health trends experienced by low-income white households have also been documented among Native Americans and Native Alaskans. See Meredith Shiels et al., "Trends in Premature Mortality in the USA by Sex, Race, and Ethnicity from 1999 to 2014: An Analysis of Death Certificate Data," *Lancet* 389.10073 (2017): 1043–54.

29. Ruth Wilson Gilmore, *Golden Gulag* (Los Angeles: University of California Press, 2007), 27.

30. Nikhil Pal Singh and Thuy Linh Tu, "Morbid Capitalism and Its Racial Symptoms," *n+1*, no. 30 (Winter 2018), https://nplusonemag.com/ issue-30/essays/morbid-capitalism/.

31. James Baldwin, "On Being White and Other Lies," *Essence Magazine*, April 1984.

32. George Lipsitz, *The Possessive Investment in Whiteness: How White People Profit from Identity Politics* (Philadelphia: Temple University Press, 1998), vii.

33. Rakesh Kochhar and Anthony Cilluffo, "How Wealth Inequality Has Changed in the U.S. since the Great Recession, by Race, Ethnicity and Income," Pew Research Center, November 1, 2017.

34. Richard J. Herrnstein and Charles Murray, *The Bell Curve* (New York: Free Press Publishing, 1994).

35. The tweet was posted on Murdoch's account on February 1, 2012, https://twitter.com/rupertmurdoch/status/164783729460510720.

36. Emphasis added. Kevin D. Williamson, "The White Ghetto," *National Review*, January 9, 2014. For a broader history of this discourse, see Kirstine Taylor, "Untimely Subjects: White Trash and the Making of Racial Innocence in the Postwar South," *American Quarterly* 67, no. 1 (2015): 55–79.

37. Williamson, "The White Ghetto," 2014.

38. Kevin Williamson, "The Father-Führer," *National Review,* March 28, 2016.

39. David French, "Working-Class Whites Have Moral Responsibilities—In Defense of Kevin Williamson," *National Review,* March 14, 2016.

40. J. D. Vance, *Hillbilly Elegy: A Memoir of a Family and Culture in Crisis* (New York: Harper, 2016), 139.

41. Vance, *Hillbilly Elegy*, 7.

42. Elizabeth Catte, "The Mythical Whiteness of Trump Country," *Boston Review*, November 7, 2017.

43. Mona Charen, "What *Hillbilly Elegy* Reveals about Trump and America," *National Review*, July 28, 2016.

44. "The Decline of the White Working Class: Featuring J. D. Vance and Charles Murray," video posted by America Enterprise Institute, YouTube, October 11, 2016, https://www.youtube.com/watch?v=Y_Idvp pb_io.

45. Robert Putnam, *Our Kids: The American Dream in Crisis* (New York: Simon & Schuster, 2015), 62.

46. Putnam, *Our Kids*, 244.

47. Harris, "Whiteness as Property."

48. Lipsitz, *The Possessive Investment in Whiteness*.

49. Leti Volpp, "Immigrants outside the Law: President Obama, Discretionary Executive Power, and Regime Change," *Critical Analysis of Law* 3 (2016): 385–404.

50. Kate Reilly, "Here Are All the Times Donald Trump Insulted Mexico," *Time*, August 31, 2016.

51. Cheryl I. Harris, "Whiteness as Property," *Harvard Law Review*, 106, no. 8 (1993): 1714.

52. Carolina Moreno, "9 Outrageous Things Donald Trump Has Said about Latinos," *Huffington Post*, November 9, 2016.

53. Jonathan T. Rothwell and Pablo Diego-Rosell, "Explaining Nationalist Political Views: The Case of Donald Trump," *SSRN*, November 2, 2016, 1.

54. Daniel Cox, Rachel Lienesch, and Robert P. Jones, "Beyond Economics: Fears of Cultural Displacement Pushed the White Working Class to Trump," *PRRI/The Atlantic Report*, May 9, 2017.

55. The *PRRI/The Atlantic* White Working Class Survey was based on phone interviews with 3,043 people in the United States conducted between September 22 and October 9, 2016.

56. Justin Gest, Tyler Reny, and Jeremy Mayer, "Roots of the Radical Right: Nostalgic Deprivation in the United States and Britain," *Comparative Political Studies* 51, no. 13 (2018): 1694–1719.

57. Shannon M. Monnat and David L. Brown, "More Than a Rural Revolt: Landscapes of Despair and the 2016 Presidential Election," *Journal of Rural Studies* 55 (2017): 231–33.

58. Carol Anderson, *White Rage: The Unspoken Truth of Our Racial Divide* (New York: Bloomsbury, 2016).

59. Email dated April 10, 2018, from "Trump Pence Make America Great Again Committee." In authors' possession.

60. Singh and Tu, "Morbid Capitalism."

61. Singh and Tu, "Morbid Capitalism."

3. *"One of Our Own"*

1. "Allen West CPAC Speech Closes Conservative Conference," *Huffington Post*, posted February 12, 2011, updated December 6, 2017.

2. Quoted in Jessica Taylor, "The Meteoric Rise of Allen West," *National Journal*, February 12, 2011.

3. "Allen West The Revolution," video posted by Channel1Images, YouTube, October 21, 2009, https://www.youtube.comwatch?v=VP2p91 dvm6M.

4. Toni Morrison, "Introduction: Friday on the Potomac," in *Racing Justice, En-Gendering Power: Essays on Anita Hill, Clarence Thomas, and the Construction of Social Reality*, ed. Toni Morrison (New York: Pantheon, 1992), vii–xix.

5. "Representative Allen West Remarks to the Conservative Political Action Conference," C-SPAN, February 12, 2011.

6. Amy Sherman, "Allen West Says about 80 House Democrats Are Members of the Communist Party," *Politifact*, April 11, 2012.

7. Jennifer Steinhauer, "Black Hopefuls Pick This Year in G.O.P. Races," *New York Times*, May 4, 2010.

8. Ryan Girdusky, "Black Republicans Could Make a Comeback in 2014," *Daily Caller*, April 24, 2014.

9. Corey D. Fields, *Black Elephants in the Room: The Unexpected Politics of African American Republicans* (Oakland: University of California Press, 2017); Joshua Farrington, *Black Republicans and the Transformation of the GOP* (Philadelphia: University of Pennsylvania Press, 2016); Timothy N. Thurber, *Republicans and Race: The GOP's Frayed Relationship with African Americans, 1945–1974* (Lawrence: University Press of Kansas, 2013); Leah Wright Rigueur, *The Loneliness of the Black Republican: Pragmatic Politics and the Pursuit of Power* (Princeton: Princeton University Press, 2015); Angela Dillard, *Guess Who's Coming to Dinner Now? Multicultural Conservatism in America* (New York: New York University Press, 2001). See also Michael L. Ondaatje, *Black Conservative Intellectuals in Modern America* (Philadelphia: University of Pennsylvania Press, 2010); Cornel West, "Demystifying the New Black Conservatism," in *Race Matters* (Boston: Beacon Press, 1993), 33–46; and Andrea Simpson, *The Tie That Binds: Identity and Political Attitudes in the Post–Civil Rights Generation* (New York: New York University Press, 1998).

10. Dillard, *Guess Who's Coming to Dinner Now?*

11. *Trends in Party Affiliation among Demographic Groups,* Pew Research Center, March 20, 2018.

12. Rigueur, *Loneliness of the Black Republican,* 2.

13. Philip Bump, "There Are Likely Fewer Black Delegates to the Republican Convention Than at Any Point in At Least a Century," *Washington Post,* July 19, 2016.

14. Two other Black Republicans have served in the House since the 1980s—Gary A. Franks in Connecticut and J. C. Watts in Oklahoma. See Adolph Reed Jr., "The Puzzle of Black Republicans," *New York Times,* December 18, 2012.

15. Rigueur, *Loneliness of the Black Republican.*

16. Victoria Hattam and Joseph Lowndes make a similar point in regard to Condoleezza Rice's use of the civil rights movement to defend the Iraq War when she was in the George W. Bush administration. See "From Birmingham to Baghdad: The Micropolitics of Regime Change," in *Political Creativity: New Approaches to Institutional Diversity and Change,* ed. Gerald Berk, Dennis Galvan, and Victoria Hattam (Philadelphia: University of Pennsylvania Press, 2013), 211–35.

17. See Manisha Sinha, *The Counterrevolution of Slavery: Politics and Ideology in Antebellum South Carolina* (Chapel Hill: University of North Carolina Press, 2000).

18. Zev Chafets, "Tim Scott: Black Republican Tea Party Favorite," *Newsweek,* November 7, 2010.

19. Nancy Weiss, *Farewell to the Party of Lincoln* (Princeton: Princeton University Press, 1983).

20. David A. Bositis, *Blacks and the 2004 Democratic National Convention* (Washington, D.C.: Joint Center for Political and Economic Studies, 2004), 9, table 1.

21. Quoted in Jason Horowitz, "Rudy's New South Carolina Co-chair," *New York Observer,* June 25, 2007.

22. "Thurmond Says He'll Seek First District Congressional Seat," *South Carolina Now,* January 20, 2010.

23. Jonathan Martin, "Paul Thurmond Charts His Course," *Politico,* February 25, 2010.

24. Scott secured 46,884 votes (68 percent) to Thurmond's 21,706 votes (32 percent). *New York Times,* December 10, 2008, https://www.nytimes.com/elections/2010/results/primaries/south-carolina.html.

25. "South Carolina Election Results." *New York Times,* December 17, 2014, https://www.nytimes.com/elections/2014/south-carolina-elections.

26. Scott Huffman, H. Gibbs Knots, and Seth McGee, "History Made: The Rise of Republican Tim Scott," *PS: Political Science & Politics*, July 2016.

27. "Council Hopes to End Commandments Suit," *Augusta Chronicle*, August 16, 1998.

28. Andrew Shain, "12 Things about Tim Scott," *The State*, December 12, 2012.

29. Yvonne Wenger, "Scott Touts S.C.'s Right-to-Work Status," *Post and Courier*, November 26, 2009; Associated Press, "S.C. Selects Black GOP Congressman; 1st since 2003," *Washington Post*, November 2, 2010.

30. Quoted in Alex Isenstadt, "Palin Backs Scott," *Politico*, June 19, 2010.

31. Scott Keyes, "Meet Sen. Tim Scott: The Tea Party Lawmaker Who Wanted to Impeach President Obama and Kick Kids off Food Stamps," *Think Progress*, December 17, 2012.

32. Huffman, Knots, and McGee, "History Made," 407.

33. Huffman, Knots, and McGee, "History Made," 410

34. M. V. Hood and Seth C. McKee, "True Colors: White Conservative Support for Minority Republican Candidates," *Public Opinion Quarterly* 79, no. 1 (January 2015): 28.

35. Huffman, Knots, and McGee, "History Made," 407.

36. Huffman, Knots, and McGee, "History Made," 407.

37. Ben Terris, "The Undercover Senator: Tim Scott Goes Anecdote Shopping in South Carolina," *Washington Post*, May 7, 2014.

38. Quoted in Louise Radnofsky, "GOP's Tim Scott Pulls Ahead in S.C. House Primary," *Wall Street Journal Blog*, June 8, 2012.

39. Quoted in Robert Behre, "Scott Easily Defeats Thurmond for GOP Nod," *Post and Courier*, June 22, 2010.

40. Quin Hillyer, "Tim Scott's Freedom Fries," *Washington Times*, August 6, 2010; David Brody, "Exclusive Tim Scott Interview: No Racism in Tea Party," *CBN Blogs*, September 21, 2010.

41. Chafets, "Tim Scott."

42. Quoted in Tim Alberta, "'God Made Me Black on Purpose,'" *Politico Magazine*, March/April 2018.

43. "Tim Scott Speaks at the Tea Party Convention, Posted by WPDE ABC 15," YouTube, January 13, 2013, https://www.youtube.com/watch?v=_UfwUP7vpwA.

44. "Tim Scott Remarks at Conservative Political Action Conference," C-SPAN, March 14, 2013.

45. "Tim Scott Remarks."

46. "Tim Scott Remarks"; emphasis added.

47. Lester K. Spence, *Knocking the Hustle: Against the Neoliberal Turn in Black Politics* (Brooklyn: Punctum Books, 2015).

48. Dillard, *Guess Who's Coming to Dinner Now?*

49. Reed, "The Puzzle of Black Republicans."

50. "Scott Plays Up Modest Background, Downplays Race," *Twin Cities Pioneer Press,* December 17, 2012, updated November 10, 2015.

51. Quoted in Chafets, "Tim Scott."

52. Quoted in Alberta, "'God Made Me Black On Purpose.'"

53. Conor Friedersdorf, "The Senate's Only Black Republican Opens Up about Being Mistreated by Cops," *Atlantic,* July 15, 2016, https://www.theatlantic.com/politics/archive/2016/07/the-senates-only-black-republican-opens-up-about-being-mistreated-by-police/491435/.

54. In 2017, Scott introduced a bill to create a database of police shootings, named the Walter Scott Notification Act. Ted Barrett, "Tim Scott Chokes Up on Senate floor Remembering Shooting Victims," CNN, Thursday 25, 2015.

55. James H. Kuklinski, Michael D. Cobb, and Martin Gilens, "Racial Attitudes and the 'New South,'" *Journal of Politics* 59, no. 2 (1997): 323–49; Matthew D. Luttig, Christopher M. Federico, and Howard Lavine, "Supporters and Opponents of Donald Trump Respond Differently to Racial Cues: An Experimental Analysis," *Research and Politics* 4, no. 4 (2017): 1–8; Brenda Major, Alison Blodorn, and Gregor Major Blascovich, "The Threat of Increasing Diversity: Why Many White Americans Support Trump in the 2016 Presidential Election," *Group Processes and Intergroup Relations* 21, no. 6 (2016): 931–40. On Tea Party voters and race more generally, see Christopher S. Parker and Matt Barretto, *Change They Can't Believe In: The Tea Party and Reactionary Politics in America* (Princeton: Princeton University Press, 2013).

56. Cameron Easley, "America's Most and Least Popular Senators," *Morning Consult,* January 23, 2018.

57. "Mia Love RNC Speech," text and video, *Politico,* August 20, 2012.

58. Diane Jeanty, "Mia Love's Victory Met with Little Enthusiasm in Her Own Haitian Community," *Huffington Post,* November 14, 2014; Mary C Curtis, "Mia Love is Black, Mormon, Republican, and Blowing People's Minds," *Washington Post,* November 12, 2014, https://www.washingtonpost.com/blogs/she-the-people/wp/2014/11/12/mia-love-is-black-mormon-republican-and-blowing-peoples-minds/?utm_term=.5d3598ca7a1e.

59. "Mia Love RNC Speech."

60. Alexis Levinson, "'Love Bomb' Showers Utah Candidate with $100K after RNC Speech," *Daily Caller,* August 29, 2012.

61. "Mia Love Rejects CNN's Race Card," YouTube, November 5, 2014, https://www.youtube.com/watch?v=VfjwKG3o4wY; "Mia Love RNC Speech."

62. "Representative Mia Love (R-UT) Remarks at CPAC 2015," C-SPAN, February 26, 2015.

63. "Representative Mia Love Remarks."

64. "Representative Mia Love Remarks."

65. "Tea Party Endorses Mia Love for Congress in UT-4," Tea Party Express, http://www.teapartyexpress.org/8675/tea-party-express-endorses-mia-love-for-congress-in-ut-4; Alyssa Canobbio, "Mia Love Delivers Heartfelt Speech at March for Life," *Washington Free Beacon*, January 27, 2017; Jason Linkins, "Mia Love Just Wants Everyone at CPAC to Be Confident," video and text, *Huffington Post*, March 16, 2013. In 2018, Love faced no Republican challenger in the primary but lost her seat in the general election by a narrow margin to Democrat Ben McAdams, the mayor of Salt Lake City.

66. Love disavowed the group's efforts and endorsement. Courtney Tanner, "A Group That Supported Roy Moore Is Now Raising Thousands for Utah Rep. Mia Love to Run for U.S. Senate—and Stop Mitt Romney," *Salt Lake Tribune*, January 4, 2015.

67. Adolph L. Reed, "Black Particularity Reconsidered," *Telos* 39 (Spring 1979): 72.

68. Reed, "Black Particularity Reconsidered," 72, 74, 78.

69. Rigueur, *Loneliness of the Black Republican*, 4.

70. Quoted in Farrington, *Black Republicans*, 186–87.

71. Quoted in Theodore R. Johnson, "What Nixon Can Teach the GOP about Courting Black Voters," *Politico*, August 15, 2015.

72. Reed, "Black Particularity Reconsidered," 84.

73. Reed, "Black Particularity Reconsidered," 85.

74. Cedric Johnson, *Revolutionaries to Race Leaders: Black Power and the Making of African American Politics* (Minneapolis: University of Minnesota Press, 2007).

75. Reed, "Black Particularity Reconsidered," 92.

76. Roderick Ferguson, *Aberrations in Black*: *Toward a Queer of Color Critique* (Minneapolis: University of Minnesota Press, 2004).

77. Stuart Hall, "New Ethnicities," in *Black Film/British Cinema* (London: Institute of Contemporary Arts, 1988), 433–34.

78. Matthew Dallek, "Donald Trump Is the Ultimate Republican Repudiation of Jack Kemp's Legacy," *Washington Post*, May 12, 2016.

79. Quoted in "The Republicans; Bush Outlines His Goals: 'I Want to Change the Tone of Washington,'" *New York Times,* August 4, 2000.

80. President George W. Bush, speech, NAACP annual convention, Washington, D.C., July 20, 2006.

81. Adolph Reed Jr., *Stirrings in the Jug: Black Politics in the Post-segregation Era* (Minneapolis: University of Minnesota Press, 1999).

82. Toni Morrison, "Comment," *New Yorker,* October 5, 1998.

83. Michelle Alexander, "Why Hillary Clinton Doesn't Deserve the Black Vote," *Nation,* February 10, 2016.

84. Alana Semuels, "The End of Welfare as We Know It: America's Once-Robust Safety Net Is No More," *Atlantic,* April 1, 2016.

85. Francis X. Clines, "Clinton Signs Bill Cutting Welfare; States in New Role," *New York Times,* August 23, 1996.

86. Christopher Petrella, "On Stone Mountain," *Boston Review,* March 30, 2016.

87. "Remarks by the First Lady at Martin Luther King Jr. Preparatory High School Commencement Address," June 9, 2015, https://obama whitehouse.archives.gov.

88. Eliana Johnson and Nancy Cook, "The Real Reason Jim DeMint Got the Boot," *Politico,* May 2, 2017; Jennifer Steinhauer and Jonathan Weisman, "In the DeMint Era at Heritage, a Shift from Policy to Politics," *New York Times,* February 23, 2014.

89. Jeremy W. Peters, "Heritage Foundation Names New President after Turmoil under DeMint," *New York Times,* December 19, 2017.

90. Kay Coles James, "I'm an African-American Woman: Here's My Advice to Conservatives Wooing my Community," *Daily Signal,* August 29, 2016.

91. Paul Krugman, "For God's Sake," *New York Times,* April 13, 2007.

92. They were the Office of Management and Budget, the Office of Personnel Management, and the General Services Administration. Edwin Feulner and Kay James, "Kay Coles James Addresses Heritage Staff," Heritage Foundation, December 19, 2017.

93. Quoted in Rob Bluey, "Kay Coles James to Lead the Heritage Foundation as Next President," *Daily Signal,* December 19, 2017.

94. "The Gloucester Institute: About," https://www.gloucesterinsti tute.org/about.

95. James, "I'm an African-American Woman."

96. Feulner and James, "Kay Coles James Addresses Heritage Staff."

97. Breitbart News Daily—Kay Coles James, March 6, 2018, https://soundcloud.com/breitbart/breitbart-news-daily-kay-coles-james-march-6-2018.

4. *"A Brown Brother for Donald Trump"*

1. Gary Gerstle, *American Crucible: Race and Nation in the Twentieth Century* (Princeton: Princeton University Press, 2002); Rogers Smith, *Civic Ideals: Conflicting Visions of Citizenship in U.S. History* (New Haven, Conn.: Yale University Press, 1997).

2. Quoted in Robert Kuttner, "Steve Bannon, Unrepentant," *American Prospect*, August 16, 2017.

3. Nina Burleigh, "The Bannon Canon: Books Favored by the Trump Adviser," *Newsweek*, March 23, 2017.

4. "Steve Bannon: 5 Things to Know," Anti-Defamation League, https://www.adl.org/resources/backgrounders/steve-bannon-five-things-to-know, podcast.

5. "Steve Bannon's War," *The Daily*, *New York Times*, November 10, 2017, podcast.

6. Quoted in Selena Hill, "Steve Bannon Lectures Black Businesses on 'Economic Nationalism,'" *Black Enterprise*, November 13, 2017.

7. Quoted in Adelle Nazarian, "Steve Bannon Headlines Fundraiser for Black, Minority Entrepreneurs," Breitbart News, December 4, 2017.

8. "Steve Bannon's War."

9. Michael Rogin, "The Two Declarations of American Independence," *Representations*, no. 55 (July 1996): 13.

10. Philip J. Deloria, *Playing Indian* (New Haven, Conn.: Yale University Press, 1999); Richard Slotkin, *Regeneration through Violence: The Mythology of the American Frontier* (Norman: University of Oklahoma Press, 1973).

11. Frederick Jackson Turner, "The Significance of the Frontier in American History" (Ann Arbor: University Microfilms, 1966).

12. James Baldwin, *The Price of the Ticket: Collected Nonfiction, 1948–1985* (New York: St. Martin's/Marek, 1985); Toni Morrison, *Playing in the Dark: Whiteness and the Literary Imagination* (Cambridge, Mass.: Harvard University Press, 1992); Eric Lott, *Love and Theft: Blackface Minstrelsy and the American Working Class* (New York: Oxford University Press, 1993).

13. "White Nationalist Reggae?" posting, June 4, 2011, Stormfront, https://www.stormfront.org/forum/t806562/.

14. Carroll Smith-Rosenberg, "Dis-Covering the Subject of the 'Great Constitutional Discussion,' 1786–1789," in "Discovering America," special issue, *Journal of American History* 79, no. 3 (December 1992): 848.

15. Quoted in David Weigel, "Trump Rallies Thousands in Mississippi with Anger at Media, Iran Deal," *Washington Post*, January 2, 2016.

16. Quoted in Joseph E. Lowndes, "From Silent Majority to White-Hot Rage: Observations from Cleveland," *CounterPunch*, July 22, 2016.

17. "Jamiel Shaw Sr. Speaks at Republican National Convention (7–18–16)," video posted by Right Side Broadcasting Network, YouTube, July 18, 2016, https://www.youtube.com/watch?v=n6KHBnNKlIY.

18. "Trade War with China Is Bad, U.S. Voters Say 3-1, Quinnipiac University National Poll Finds; Voters Support National Guard, But Not the Wall," *Quinnipiac University Poll*, April 11, 2018.

19. See, for example, Tatishe Nteta, "United We Stand? African Americans, Self-Interest, and Immigration Reform," *American Politics Research* 41, no. 1 (2013): 147–72.

20. "The Federation for American Immigration Reform Creates Black Front Group," *Intelligence Report*, Southern Poverty Law Center, October 19, 2006; "Anti-immigrant Front Groups Used in Fight against Immigration Reform," Anti-Defamation League, May 3, 2013; Michelle Cottle, "The Shady Group behind the African-American Anti-immigration Rally," *Daily Beast*, July 12, 2013.

21. "Extremist Files/Federation for American Immigration Reform," Southern Poverty Law Center, https://www.splcenter.org/fighting-hate/extremist-files/group/federation-american-immigration-reform. FAIR has initiated several formations, including the Black American Leadership Alliance, the African American Leadership Council, Choose Black America, and the Coalition for the Future American Worker, to suggest that Black public opinion favors immigration restriction. Cottle, "The Shady Group."

22. Claire Jean Kim, *Bitter Fruit: The Politics of Black-Korean Conflict in New York City* (New Haven, Conn.: Yale University Press, 2000).

23. "Why You Lost Part 1—He Will Not Divide Us," video posted by Trump Patriot, YouTube, March 18, 2017, https://www.youtube.com/watch?v=OuidHYtjphg.

24. "Asian Trump Supporter Smashes Liberals and Identity Politics," YouTube, February 6, 2017, https://www.youtube.com/watch?v=HI-VD2bgGeM.

25. Charles Dickens, *A Christmas Carol*. (London: Wordsworth Classics, 1993), 62.

26. Quoted in Benny Luo, "Meet the Trump Fan Who Wants Liberals to Suck His 'Big Asian Cock,'" *Nextshark*, February 17, 2017.

27. Abigail Hauslohner, Paul Duggan, Jack Gillum, and Aaron C. Davis, "James Fields Jr.: A Neo-Nazi's Violent, Rage-Fueled Journey to Charlottesville," *Chicago Tribune*, August 18, 2017.

28. Matt Labash, "A Beating in Berkeley," *Weekly Standard*, September 11, 2017, https://www.weeklystandard.com/matt-labash/a-beating-in-berkeley.

29. Quoted in Labash, "A Beating in Berkeley."

30. Brendan Hokowhitu, "Haka: Colonialized Physicality, Body Logic, and Embodied Sovereignty," in *Performing Indigeneity: Global Histories and Contemporary Experiences,* ed. Laura R. Graham and H. Glenn Penny (Lincoln: University of Nebraska Press, 2014), 273–304.

31. Live feed from Tiny John Toese's public Facebook page, November 25, 2018. Last viewed December 5, 2018.

32. Matthew N. Lyons, *Ctrl-Alt-Delete: The Origins and Ideology of the Alternative Right,* Political Research Associates, January 20, 2017.

33. Gavin McInnes, "We Are Not Alt-Right: The Founder Goes on Record," *Proud Boy Magazine*, August 21, 2017.

34. Quoted in Hatewatch Staff, "Do You Want Bigots, Gavin? Because This Is How You Get Bigots," Southern Poverty Law Center, August 10, 2017.

35. Quoted in George Hawley, *Making Sense of the Alt-Right* (New York: Columbia University Press, 2017), 150.

36. Samuel Francis, *Essential Writings on Race,* (Oakton, Va.: New Century Books, 2007) 18–19.

37. Quoted in Paul Nehlen, "Diamond and Silk Are Simply the Best: They Are Ready to #DumpRyan," video on Facebook, August 5, 2016. Oscar Mayer's parent company, Kraft, had recently announced a plan to close a longtime Madison, Wisconsin–based facility. Brad Reed, "Flashback: Trump Supporters Diamond and Silk Were Paid $7K to Cut Campaign Ad for Wisconsin Neo-Nazi," *Raw Story*, April 26, 2018.

38. Brad Reed, "Diamond and Silk Busted for Lying under Oath about Trump Payments as Their House Hearing Goes off the Rails," *Raw Story*, April 26, 2018.

5. State Abandonment and Militia Revolt

1. Brian Jennings, Sherron Lumley, and Corinne Boyer, "Anarchy in Eastern Oregon—Don't Tread on Me," *Bend Source*, January 13, 2016.

2. Donnell Alexander, "The Darkness in Burns, Oregon," *Rolling Stone*, February 4, 2016.

3. Ryan J. Gallagher, Andrew J. Reagan, Christopher M. Danforth, and Peter Sheridan Dodds, "Divergent Discourse between Protests and Counter-Protests: #BlackLivesMatter and #AllLivesMatter," *PLoS ONE* 13, no. 4 (April 18, 2018). See also Keeanga-Yamahtta Taylor, *From #BlackLivesMatter to Black Liberation* (Chicago: Haymarket Books, 2016).

4. John Vibes, "Black Lives Matter Teams Up with Oregon Occupier Supporters to Fight for Police Accountability," The Free Thought Project, February 18, 2016, https://thefreethoughtproject.com/black-lives-matter-teams-oregon-occupiers-fight-police-accountability/.

5. Robin D. G. Kelley, "Beyond Black Lives Matter," *Kalfou* 2, no. 2 (Fall 2015): 332–33.

6. Quoted in Adam Nagourney, "A Defiant Rancher Savors the Audience That Rallied to His Side," *New York Times*, April 23, 2014.

7. Bryan Denson, "Controversial Oregon Ranchers in Court Wednesday, Likely Headed Back to Prison in Arson Case," *The Oregonian*/Oregon Live, October 7, 2015.

8. Constitutional Sheriffs and Peace Officers Association quoted in Mark Potok and Ryan Lenz, *Line in the Sand*, Southern Poverty Law Center Intelligence Report, June 13, 2016.

9. On rural militia activities and white supremacy see Chip Berlet and Matthew N. Lyons, *Right-Wing Populism in America: Too Close for Comfort* (New York: Guilford Press, 2000); Beverly Brown, *In Timber Country: Working Peoples' Stories of Environmental Conflict and Urban Flight* (Philadelphia: Temple University Press, 1995); Sara Diamond, *Roads to Dominion: Right-Wing Movements and Political Power in the United States* (New York: Guilford Press, 1995); Arlene Stein, *The Stranger Next Door: The Story of a Small Community's Battle over Sex, Faith, and Civil Rights* (Boston: Beacon Press, 2001); Kenneth Stern, *A Force upon the Plain: The American Militia Movement and the Politics of Hate* (New York: Simon & Schuster, 1996); Nelle Van Dyke and Sarah A. Soule, "Structural Social Change and the Mobilizing Effect of Threat: Explaining Levels of Patriot and Militia Organizing in the United States," *Social Problems* 49, no. 4 (2002): 497–520.

10. Ammon Bundy "Dear Friends," YouTube, January 1, 2016, https://www.youtube.com/watch?v=M7M0mG6HUyk&t=488s.

11. Spencer Sunshine with Rural Organizing Project and Political Research Associates, *Up in Arms: A Guide to Oregon's Patriot Movement*

(Somerville, Mass.: Political Research Associates, 2016), http://www.rop
.org/wp-content/uploads/Up-in-Arms_Report_PDF-1.pdf.

12. Sarah Cate and Daniel HoSang, "'The Better Way to Fight Crime': Why Fiscal Arguments Do Not Restrain the Carceral State," *Theoretical Criminology* 22, no. 2 (2018): 169–88.

13. Thena Robinson Mock, Ruth Jeannoel, Rachel Gilmer, Chelsea Fuller, and Marbre Stahly-Butts, "End the War on Black People," The Movement for Black Lives website, https://policy.m4bl.org/end-war-on
-black-people/.

14. On the Partnership for Safety and Justice, see https://safetyand
justice.org/.

15. Molly Young, "Behind the Harney County Standoff, Decades of Economic Decline," *The Oregonian*/Oregon Live, January 14, 2016, updated February 22, 2016.

16. Steven Beda, "Landscapes of Solidarity: Timber Workers and the Making of Place in the Pacific Northwest, 1900–1964" (PhD diss., University of Washington, 2014). See also Erik Loomis, *Empire of Timber: Labor Unions and the Pacific Northwest Forests* (New York: Cambridge University Press), 2015.

17. Chuck Willer, "A Colony Called Oregon," Coast Range Associates, 2017, http://coastrange.org/JuneCRALetter_2017forCRAwebsite/
JuneCRALetter_2017forCRAwebsite.html. The analysis was done on forest ownership in western Oregon in particular, but it reflects ownership trends throughout the state.

18. Young, "Behind the Harney County Standoff."

19. Patricia Cohen and Robert Gebeloff, "Public Servants Are Losing Their Foothold in the Middle Class," *New York Times*, April 22, 2018.

20. Quoted in Ian Kullgren, "Burns Paiute Tribe: Militants Need to Get off 'Our Land,'" *The Oregonian*/Oregon Live, January 6, 2016; Kelly House, "Burns Paiutes to Ammon Bundy: You're Not the Victim," *The Oregonian*/Oregon Live, February 7, 2016, updated February 23, 2016.

21. Burns Paiute Tribe, "Our Mission," Burns Paiute Natural Resources, https://www.burnspaiute-nsn.gov/index.php/departments/natural
-resources.

22. Peter Walker, *Sagebrush Collaboration* (Corvallis: Oregon State University Press, 2018).

23. Scott Learn, "Rough and Ready Lumber, Josephine County's Last Sawmill, a Casualty of Southwest Oregon's Enduring Timber Wars," *The Oregonian*/Oregon Live, May 20, 2013.

24. Phillip A. Neel, *Hinterland: America's New Landscape of Class and Conflict* (Chicago: University of Chicago Press, 2018).

25. Quoted in Stephanie McNeal, "Citizens Take Law into Own Hands after Cash-Strapped Oregon County Guts Sheriff's Office," Fox News, December 28, 2013.

26. Associated Press, "Laid-off Deputy Trains Armed Group How to Respond to Crime in Josephine County after Budget Cuts," *The Oregonian*/Oregon Live, February 14, 2013.

27. Michelle Brence, "Voters Reject 2 Public Safety Measures: Oregon Election Roundup," *The Oregonian*/Oregon Live, May 20, 2015.

28. Quoted in Clara Jeffrey and Monika Bauerlein, "The Job Killers," *Mother Jones*, November/December 2011, https://www.motherjones.com/politics/2011/10/republicans-job-creation-kill/.

29. James Pogues, "The Oath Keepers Are Ready for War with the Federal Government," *Vice*, September 14, 2015.

30. Walter Johnson, "What Do We Mean When We Say, 'Structural Racism'? A Walk down West Florissant Avenue, Ferguson, Missouri," *Kalfou* 3, no. 1 (2016): 36–62; "Platform" of the Movement for Black Lives, https://policy.m4bl.org/platform/. See also Taylor, *From #Black LivesMatter to Black Liberation*. For a more sober account of the challenges facing organizers in Ferguson, see Neel, *Hinterland*, chapter 5.

31. Michael Paul Rogin, "The Countersubversive Tradition in American Politics," *Berkeley Journal of Sociology* 31 (1986): 1–33.

32. Aaron Morrison, "Oregon Standoff Leader: 'There Is Probably Some Similarities' to Black Lives Matter Movement," *International Business Times*, January 4, 2016, http://www.ibtimes.com/oregon-standoff-leader-there-probably-some-similarities-black-lives-matter-movement-2248094.

33. Eileen Sullivan and Julie Turkewitz, "Trump Pardons Oregon Ranchers Whose Case Inspired Wildlife Refuge Takeover," *New York Times*, July 10, 2018, https://www.nytimes.com/2018/07/10/us/politics/trump-pardon-hammond-oregon.html.

34. Raúl M. Grijalva, "With Hammond Pardons, Did Donald Trump Write a Blank Check to Anti-government Extremists?" *USA Today*, July 18, 2018.

Conclusion

1. The video was posted on Patriot Prayer's Facebook page on June 3, 2018, https://www.facebook.com/100013660111371/videos/437348

323397168/?hc_ref=ARSA5lk_cmaVqJOMTR-EkoyI_sQxOGyd6aV8q puLoi_1SN1tMt4m7_ptN-mhSWeZ-QA. The speaker's comments begin at the 7:55 mark.

2. Jason Wilson, "Far-Right Group Brawls with Anti-fascist Protesters in Portland Streets," June 4, 2018, https://www.theguardian.com/ world/2018/jun/04/patriot-prayer-proud-boys-antifa-fights-brawls-port land.

3. Shane Burley, *Fascism Today: What It Is and How to End It* (Chico, Calif.: AK Press, 2017).

4. Wilson, "Far-Right Group Brawls."

5. "'Pinochet Did No Wrong': Who Is Pinochet?" KOIN 6, August 4, 2018, https://www.koin.com/news/local/multnomah-county/-pinochet -did-no-wrong-who-is-pinochet-/1346777062.

6. "The Legend of Tiny Toese: American Samoan Patriot," video from August 13, 2017, Patriot Prayer rally in Seattle, Washington; Arlie Hochschild, *Strangers in Their Own Land: Anger and Mourning on the American Right* (New York: New Press, 2016).

7. Joey Gibson, interview with the authors, April 29, 2018; "Joey Gibson US Senate," https://gibsonforfreedom.com/.

8. See Alexander Reid Ross, *Against the Fascist Creep* (Chico, Calif.: AK Press, 2017).

9. "Steve Bannon Remarks to Minority Entrepreneur Conference," C-SPAN, December 5, 2017, https://www.c-span.org/video/?438151-1/ steve-bannon-addresses-minority-entrepreneurs-conference.

10. Danielle Kurtzleben, "Here's How Many Bernie Sanders Supporters Ultimately Voted for Trump," NPR, August 24, 2017.

11. The comments are taken from "We Are Breitbart," promotional video published by Breitbart News, YouTube, March 4, 2017, https:// www.youtube.com/watch?v=PvDpivo68jU. A list of the 2016 meetups can be found at http://www.breitbart.com/meetups/.

12. Victoria Hattam and Joseph Lowndes, "The Ground beneath Our Feet: Language, Culture and Political Change," in *Formative Acts: American Politics in the Making*, ed. Steven Skowronek and Matthew Glassman (Philadelphia: University of Pennsylvania Press, 2007), 204.

13. Aziz Rana, "Goodbye, Cold War," *n+1*, no. 30 (Winter 2018), https://nplusonemag.com/issue-30/politics/goodbye-cold-war/.

14. Donald L. Warren, *The Radical Center: Middle Americans and the Politics of Alienation* (South Bend, Ind.: University of Notre Dame Press, 1976), xx.

15. Thomas Byrne Edsall and Mary Edsall, *Chain Reaction: The Impact of Race, Rights, and Taxes on American Politics* (New York: Norton, 1992).

16. Ruy Teixeira and Joel Rogers, *America's Forgotten Majority: Why the White Working Class Still Matters* (New York: Basic Books, 2001).

17. Jess Manuel Krogstad, *2016 Electorate Will Be the Most Diverse in U.S. History,* Pew Research Center, February 3, 2016.

18. Joan C. Williams, "What So Many People Don't Get about the U.S. Working Class," *Harvard Business Review*, November 10, 2016.

19. Arlie Hochschild, *Strangers in Their Own Land: Anger and Mourning on the American Right* (New York: New Press, 2016).

20. Had Hochschild wanted to grasp what produced the politics of her subjects she might have reflected on the Republican gubernatorial campaign of Klansman David Duke in 1991, or further back Goldwater's racially charged victory in 1964—the first time ever that the state went Republican for a presidential candidate, or even further back the role that legendary Plaquemines Parish political boss Leander Perez played in the Dixiecrat Revolt of 1948—all of which shape the kinds of contemporary political identifications she seeks to understand. For that matter, the political orientation of these Louisiana Tea Partiers may also be rooted in alternate histories that disobey the narrative of class and race resentment, such as the 1887 biracial strike by cane cutters in Thibodaux that ended in the massacre of hundreds by the state militia, or Huey Long's immensely popular populist attacks on elites in the 1930s. On Perez and Louisiana's role in the Dixiecrat Revolt of 1948 see Glenn Jeansonne, *Leander Perez: Boss of the Delta* (Lexington: University of Mississippi Press, 2006). On the Goldwater campaign of 1964 see Joseph Lowndes, *From the New Deal to the New Right: Race and the Southern Origins of Modern Conservatism* (New Haven, Conn.: Yale University Press, 2008), chapters 2 and 3. On the sugar strike of 1897 see Alex Gourevitch, *From Slavery to the Cooperative Commonwealth: Labor and Republican Liberty in the Nineteenth Century* (New York: Cambridge University Press, 2015).

21. William Graham Sumner, *Folkways: A Study of the Sociological Importance of Usages, Manners, Customs, Mores and Morals* (New York: Ginn, 1906). Another articulation of this thesis can be found in social psychology; see John Turner and Penny Oakes, "The Significance of the Social Identity Concept for Social Psychology with Reference to Individualism, Interactionism and Social Influence," *British Journal of Social Psychology* 25, no. 3 (1986): 237–52.

22. Amy Chua, *Political Tribes: Group Instinct and the Fate of Nations* (New York: Penguin, 2018), 4.

23. Thomas B. Edsall, "Liberals Need to Take Their Fingers Out of Their Ears," *New York Times*, December 7, 2017; David Brooks, "The Retreat to Tribalism," *New York Times,* January 1, 2018.

24. Ed Mazza, "Vanilla ISIS & Y'All Qaeda: Oregon Gunmen Mocked on Social Media," *Huffington Post*, January, 4, 2016.

25. Chua, *Political Tribes*, 208, 209. Chua's remedies seem in many ways to be a rehashing of the "Americans All" movement of the 1930s, which sought national redemption through a respect for cultural pluralism. See, for example, Diana Selig, *Americans All: The Cultural Gifts Movement* (Cambridge, Mass.: Harvard University Press, 2011). These efforts placed much greater emphasis on building the national unity necessary for wartime mobilizations and militarism, but they left actual structures of racial domination (such as Jim Crow) in place.

26. Phil A. Neel, *Hinterland: America's New Landscape of Class and Conflict* (London: Reaktion Books, 2018).

27. Dr. Martin Luther King Jr., "MLK Public Statement on the Poor People's Campaign," December 4, 1967, 1, 3, http://www.thekingcenter.org/archive/document/mlk-public-statement-poor-peoples-campaign.

28. Thanks to Malori Musselman for the political assertion, in response to a presentation of this project, that "we are all parasites."

29. King, "MLK Public Statement," 4.

30. Sylvia Laurent, *King and the Other America: The Poor People's Campaign and the Quest for Economic Equality* (Berkeley: University of California Press, 2018); William J. Barber II and Jonathan Wilson-Hartgrove, *The Third Reconstruction: How a Moral Movement Is Overcoming the Politics of Division and Fear* (Boston: Beacon Press, 2016); Gordon K. Mantler, *Power to the Poor: Black-Brown Coalition and the Fight for Economic Justice, 1960–1974* (Chapel Hill: University of North Carolina Press, 2015).

31. George Lipsitz, "'What Kind of Ally Are You?' Intersectional Activism and Social Analysis," June 2018, (unpublished manuscript in authors' possession).

32. Audre Lorde, "Learning from the 60s," in *Sister Outsider: Essays and Speeches by Audre Lorde* (Berkeley: Crossing Press, 2007), 134–44.

33. Bernice Johnson Reagon, "Coalition Politics: Turning the Century," in *Homegirls: A Black Feminist Anthology,* ed. Barbara Smith (New York: Kitchen Table: Women of Color Press, 1983), 359.

34. Lorde, "Learning from the 60s," 136.

35. Lipsitz, "'What Kind of Ally Are You?'"

36. Lorde, "Learning from the 60s," 137.

37. Fred Moten, in "The General Antagonism: An Interview with Stevphen Shukaitis," in *The Undercommons: Fugitive Planning and Black Study*, ed. Stefano Harney and Fred Moten (Wivenhoe, UK: Minor Compositions, 2013), 140–41.

38. Arlene Stein, *The Stranger Next Door* (Boston: Beacon Press, 2001).

39. See more about the Rural Organizing Project at www.rop.org.

40. A small sampling of these groups includes the Virginia Organizing Project, Kentuckians for the Commonwealth, the Highlander Center, Southerners on New Ground, the Letcher Governance Project, Down Home North Carolina, Idaho Community Action Network, Southern Echo, Native Action, and the Southwest Organizing Project.

INDEX

DANIEL MARTINEZ HoSANG is associate professor of American studies and ethnicity, race, and migration at Yale University. He is author of *Racial Propositions: Ballot Initiatives and the Making of Postwar California* and coeditor of *Racial Formation in the Twenty-first Century; Seeing Race Again: Countering Colorblindness across the Disciplines;* and *Relational Formations of Race: Theory, Method, and Practice.*

JOSEPH E. LOWNDES is associate professor of political science at the University of Oregon. He is author of *From the New Deal to the New Right: Race and the Southern Origins of Modern Conservatism* and coeditor of *Race and American Political Development.*